YOUR BLUEPRINT FOR UNLIMITED ADVENTURE

You hold in your hands *How to Win at Nintendo Games II*—the essential companion volume to the original guide to America's favorite videogame system. Jeff Rovin, the author, is an acknowledged videogaming expert, computer whiz, and the editor and publisher of *Videogaming Illustrated*. Let this book be your prime "training manual" for boosting scores, improving reflexes and coordination, and deciphering codes to an all-new series of Nintendo games, plus Tengen's game, *Gauntlet.* Detailed, up-to-the-minute, and comprehensive, it leaves enough *un*said to preserve the Nintendo system as the most exciting and challenging entertainment system available.

Now the rest is up to you. Have *you* got what it takes to master the games of masters?

HOW TO WIN AT NINTENDO® GAMES II

St. Martin's Press Mass Market titles
by Jeff Rovin

HOW TO WIN AT NINTENDO GAMES
HOW TO WIN AT NINTENDO GAMES II

Coming in 1990

HOW TO WIN AT NINTENDO GAMES III

HOW TO WIN AT NINTENDO® GAMES #2

Jeff Rovin

ALSO INCLUDES THE TENGEN GAME, *GAUNTLET*

ST. MARTIN'S PRESS/NEW YORK

How to Win at Nintendo® Games II is an unofficial guide, not endorsed by Nintendo®.

Nintendo is a registered trademark of Nintendo of America Inc.

HOW TO WIN AT NINTENDO GAMES II

ISBN: 0-312-92016-4   Can. ISBN: 0-312-92017-2

Printed in the United States of America

First St. Martin's Press mass market edition/November 1989

10 9 8 7 6 5 4 3 2

ACKNOWLEDGMENTS

Many thanks to the following, who shared their vast knowledge of Nintendo games: Ryan Quirk, Brendan Begnal, John Tomlinson, Matt Dunn, Nate Sheldon, Joey Osnoss, and the DiFate Family. Special thanks to Sam and Michael, who generously sacrificed hours of homework time to help master the games.

CONTENTS

INTRODUCTION

We're back!

Since the publication of our first book, *How to Win at Nintendo Games*—and its spectacular, still-on-sale 1989 update—new cartridges have been released and readers have written to ask for tips on some of these tough-to-beat favorites.

So here we are, with an entirely *new* collection: *How to Win at Nintendo Games II!*

You'll notice a slight change in the format this time, which we first tried with our 1989 update. In order to devote more time to actual strategies, we've cut back on data about the characters and layout. After all, you don't want just a tour guide to the Temple of Doom! You want to know exactly how Indy can whip the Ram-bunctious Mola Ram.

So—when you look up an individual game in *How to Win at Nintendo Games II,* this is what you'll find:

Type: What kind of game it is, such as fantasy quest, commando raid, space combat, sports, etc.

Objective: A short summary of what the game's about.

Layout: What the screen looks like.

Hero: All about the character's powers and weaknesses.

Enemies: A description of the major foes you'll be facing, along with their powers.

Menu: Game variations.

Scoring: What you have to do to earn points, extra heroes, more time, and so forth.

Beginner's Strategy: Tips for someone who is just starting out.

Advanced Strategy: A guide for the more experienced player.

Par: How far the average player should be able to go in the game.

Training Tips: What you can do to improve your performance in the game.

Rating: In case you don't have the cartridge, this handy buyer's guide section will tell you whether or not it's worth the money. The games are all graded A, B, C, D, and F in the following areas:

> *Challenge:* Whether or not the game is easy to master.
>
> *Graphics:* Are they terrific, just good, or worse than what your kid brother or sister can do with a box of Crayolas?
>
> *Sound Effects:* When a spaceship blows up, does it sound like it was really blasted to atoms . . . or just kind of wimped apart into little pieces?

So there you have it! New thrills await, just by turning the page, switching on the NES, and holding onto your *Seicross* motorbike. . . .

CHAPTER ONE

ADVENTURE ISLAND

Type: Fantasy quest and shoot-'em-up.

Objective: Sweet Princess Leilani has been spirited to Adventure Island in the South Pacific by the Evil Witch Doctor. Master Higgins has pursued them, determined to rescue his beloved.

Layout: The screen scrolls horizontally. There are eight Areas in all, with several levels in each. The game doesn't pause at these levels; they're simply indicated by markers with numbers on them.

Hero: Higgins has the ability to walk and jump. As he progresses, he can acquire extra Energy, weapons, and other benefits. These are described in the instructions—except for the Pots (see Scoring). You get three Higginses per game, though you can earn more at various point levels.

Enemies: There are sundry monsters (see instructions), as well as Area Bosses. Unmentioned in the instructions are Rocks on the ground, which must be leapt, and Boulders that come rolling down at you (you get 100 points for shattering each). You also aren't informed that the Cobras spit deadly venom. There is, by the way, an error in the instructions, which state that Fire is unbeatable. Not so! If you're under the protection of a Honeygirl, you can run through Fire and destroy it, earning 200 points!

Menu: There is only the one-player game.

Scoring: You earn points as well as Energy for grabbing Energy items (50 per Fruit), and points for slaying monsters (varies; see instructions). Keep your eyes on the skies as you go: Pots will appear there. Grab these for 1000 bonus points when you get 'em . . . and more at the end of the level!

Beginner's Strategy: Your first foes will be the Sneils (we kinda think they mean Snails . . . see comment in Rating). These are easy enough to leap or club with the Axe. There's a Skateboard in the second egg. Take it, but *allow the first Bird to hit you!* You'll lose the Skateboard, but that's okay. When you're struck, stand still. An Egg will appear: break it with your Axe (not with your body), and you'll get a weapon that is unheralded in the instructions: Binary Fireballs, which are far more powerful than an Axe. Head up the hill, smashing the three Boulders. The next Egg will give you a Honeygirl; when you find these guardian angels, they'll follow you for a while (usually to the start of the next level marker). When they appear, run through every enemy to kill them . . . though make sure you still leap any pits, since a fall will kill you, Honeygirl or not! At the end of the region (just before you reach the Clouds and Water), stop, turn to the left, and heave weapons in that direction. An Egg will appear with the Hudson Bee (Hudson made the game cartridge). Snatch the insect. Later, if and when you lose your last life, simply hold the joystick to the right and press start. Thanks to having caught the bee, you'll be able to continue! Note: When you reach the Totem Poles, stand between the fourth and fifth ones, and shoot the fourth one (or you can rid the screen of enemies and just wait between the poles.) A cloud will come and carry you to a bonus stage, where you can collect all kinds of goodies without being hurt.

Continuing where we left off: heading right, you'll have to leap from Cloud to ledge to Cloud. You'd be wise to skip the Egg here: it contains a Skateboard. Unless you're a seasoned player, these brakeless conveyances are going to be *very* tough to maneuver on the short Clouds.

As you leap, you're going to be confronted by the Octs, octopi that vault straight up from the water. You can shoot these for points, or you can simply jump over them. Jumping is easy: you don't even have to stop. Just move ahead at a steady, slow pace. The Octs are timed so that you'll clear them all without stopping. An Egg here (after the 2 post) contains a Honeygirl, which'll be handy to defeat the Waler that will come flying from the water at you as you jump. As you reach the end of this level, the clouds move both horizontally and vertically; worst of all, the last one drops suddenly. Get off it *fast,* or you're going in the drink . . . permanently. You'll find yourself in a cave, now get the Egg fast, before the Bassers (blue bats) arrive. When you see the Fire, stay to the left of it and wait for the Bassers. Kill them as they arrive from the right; if you don't wait for them, they'll swarm around you and slaughter you. After you clear the Fires here, you'll find an Egg with a Honeygirl. After she leaves, watch for the second orange Platform; like the last Cloud, it falls suddenly. Shortly after you pass the 5 post, an Egg will often appear; there's a Magic Ring inside. Obviously, you should get it (though we'll leave it to you to figure out what it does). When you reach the Ice stage (falling icicles), do not—repeat, *do not*—bust the Egg in here. It contains an Eggplant, which hovers above you like the Honeygirl . . . but instead of protecting you, saps your Energy *pronto, Tonto!* There's also a Skateboard Egg lying around, which you should try and get. Wheels will get you through here with welcome speed! Often an Egg will appear at the end of this level, presenting you with Binary Fireballs.

The last part of Area One, a forest, starts with Zigmos (spiders) hanging from threads and unspooling down at you. Kill them, or else move under one, wait for the next to rise, move under it, and so on. Be very alert here, though: you'll see a Red Flower on the ground. *Whenever* you pass one of these, it means that one or more Coyotes are going to run at you from the left. Make sure you turn and blast the foul furry fiends, or be ready to jump them. (Note: Often, an Egg with Milk will appear here, to replenish your Energy.) After you clear the forest, it's time to battle Boss number one. When you reach the stone chamber, rush to the right and, while leaping, *immediately* begin heaving Axes or Fireballs. In order to defeat the giant monster, you must hit it squarely in the head 10 times (you'll know you've hit it: the head briefly glows red when clobbered). The problem, here, is that the Boss will begin marching toward the left, crowding you. If it touches you, you die. And when it begins walking, the Boss heaves flame balls; if any of these touch you, you die. (You can avoid them, though, by staying close to the brute; the fire will arc over you.) You've got a few seconds before the Boss begins to move; like we said, get in those hits *fast.* By the way, you'll know without a doubt when you've won: the Boss's head falls off.

Advanced Strategy: Area Two is more of the same, only with a greater number of monsters and more troublesome ledges, Clouds, etc. For example, the last Cloud in the first level drops super fast. A few landmarks: you can get a Honeygirl right after the Springboard (the red coil) at post 2. She stays with you until 3. After post 4, watch for a Waler leaping up at you. Also, make sure your nerves are steady: the

Clouds move fast here. When you enter the cave, stay to the left and proceed steadily but slowly, shooting the Bassers and Cobras, who will appear in tandem here. It would be wise, in fact, to wait on the left and let the Bassers come for you, killing them before walking toward the Cobras on the right. In level three, when you pass post 4, watch out for the series of Skeletons (actually, just fiery skulls) that await. Again, stay to the left and move slowly. When you reach Area Two, level four, you're in another Zigmo forest . . . with a difference. A Pooter will rush at you from the right. Kill the spiders . . . but if you have no weapon, here's what you do. Walk under the Zigmos. When you pass under the third one, stop and await the Pooter. Jump it in the area between the third and fourth spiders, then continue under the next Zigmo. When you get to the area with Rocks and spiders, you can't go under the Zigmos because of the Rocks. So, jump the spiders when they're low, which will also let you clear the stones. Note: You'll be treated to two Coyotes for every Red Flower you pass here.

Coming upon a pair of Kellos (frogs), if you're still weaponless (or just want to test your maneuvering abilities), leap the first and run under the second. You'll find an Axe shortly after this section. Following another nest of Cobras, you'll face Boss two. Fight this ugly as you did the other; it's exactly the same.

Area Three is where the game hunkers

down and gets tough. The first Egg has an Axe or Milk. When you reach the brick chamber, it's more Bassers, Cobras, and moving Platforms. When you reach the first two rising and falling Platforms, get on the first whenever you want (if it hits the ceiling with you on it, you'll simply be dropped to the one beneath it). The Platform on the right will be falling; jump toward it the instant it comes down from the ceiling, and get right off of it, onto the ledge. If the Platform vanishes from the bottom of the screen and you haven't left it, you lose a Higgins. When you reach the series of horizontally-shifting Platforms, there isn't a steady rhythm you can establish that'll allow you to hop without stopping. So, get on each, wait until the Platforms (which move at different speeds) are together, then jump. There are 10 in all. When you get to the other side, watch out for the Boulder, which comes rolling toward you at once! The next series of Platforms—9 in a row—are easily taken with steady, nonstop jumping. This brings you to the end of Area Three, level one. You're now in a pastoral setting, with three Birds and two Cobras. After getting past them, the third snake you meet inaugurates a new level of pain: the Cobras henceforth spit multiple bursts of venom. To deal with this monster (which appears after the three Fires), go up the incline *slowly*. Jump the Boulder that comes rolling down, then go ahead and blast the snake. All you need do is stay on the ground and shoot it; the venom will pass over your head. With the snakes that follow, use the stationary Rocks for shelter, leaping up from behind them to fire. Note: You can hit the snakes when they are just off-screen. Watch out for the frogs here, as even after you pass them, they jump from left to right, following you. These pains *must* be slain.

In Area Three, level three, the first Egg is a Flower. There are more Clouds; watch out, as the last Oct leaps up under and through the Cloud instead of between them, like its fellows. You can cross this mess of Clouds (and avoid that nagging Oct) if you rush-jump across, never stopping. There's more forest, and then the third Boss; this one takes 12 hits in the head to kill.

Area Four offers up another forest. Hop the Snails; there's a Honeygirl in the first Egg, a Skateboard in the second. However, you'd be wise to avoid the wheels: they'll coast you right into a flock of Birds! Area Four, level two, dishes up some new scenery: white Cliffs, which you must hop up, along, and down. Boulders roll down at you and monsters attack: all are easy to deal with. Hug the right side of a Cliff step while you ascend, and moving monsters of Boulders will pass right over you. For stationary monsters, simply hop up, fire, drop back, hop again, fire, etc. Note: The Egg after post 4 usually contains Milk.

If you've gotten this far, you've got the hang of the game. Going further is up to you!

Par: A decent player should get through most of Area Two without much difficulty (earning an average of 15,000 points per Area). Going all the way requires a videogaming pro!

Training Tips: The best tip we can offer is the following. The game doesn't allow you to continue where you were killed, but tosses you back to the beginning. This isn't going to allow you to face later dangers and improve your play. Thus, when you lose your last Higgins and the screen comes back on, press the controller (or joystick) to the left, simultaneously push start . . . and you'll be able to continue at the beginning of the level at which you perished!

Rating: *Adventure Island* is a terrific game that requires a good eye and quick hand. The enemies are ingeniously situated for maximum annoyance! Our only complaint: the screens and foes become redundant after a while. As Master Higgins forges ahead, he simply moves through more crowded areas he's traversed before. Still, you'll be too busy leaping, shooting, and dodging to complain. A final comment: as we rail about later (see Rating in *ZANAC*) the Japanese-to-English translations on too many Nintendo game instructions *stink*. Bad. Spelling and grammar are godawful, and this game is a prime offender. "Loosing all energy" instead of "losing"; "as he explore the island" instead of "explores"; you earn "loopts" for killing Cobras instead of "100 pts"; and many more. We don't need im-

port quotas; we need translators who know our language.
Challenge: A
Graphics: B
Sound: B—

CHAPTER TWO

ATHENA

Type: Fantasy quest.

Objective: The Greek Goddess of Wisdom has become bored with the sedate life of an Olympian, and has decided to leave her castle, venture into the Fantasy World, and transform herself from a "mere" goddess into the Princess of Victory.

Layout: The screen scrolls horizontally, with limited vertical movement. Fantasy World is divided into a series of realms: World of Forest, World of Caverns, World of Water, and so on.

Hero: Athena can obtain a variety of weapons, most of which are detailed in the instruction booklet. What the booklet doesn't tell you, however, is that new weapons supplant old ones; don't automatically pick up a Bow and Arrow, for example, if you want to keep the Iron Ball and Chain you're swinging. (Objects uncovered in Bricks will disappear after 5 seconds.) Also, the instructions don't tell you the best weapon of all, which you get with a Magic Scroll: rapid-fire Discuses! You begin the game with one Athena on the screen and two in reserve.

Enemies: Most of the goddess's enemies are identified in the instructions—except for a few roaming beasties such as the flaming Medusa and the end-of-level supermonsters, that is, the Killer Tree, the Golem, the Fire-Octopus, and so on.

Menu: There is just the one-player quest.

Scoring: Athena collects points by defeating enemies and collecting Moneybags, and gains strength and endurance ("hit points") from finding weapons. Conversely, she loses power when she's hit, and is also racing against a clock. If time runs out, Athena dies. Two notes: You do not gain points for breaking Bricks which conceal the weapons; and, though you only have 5 minutes to get through any given World, time stops when you battle the supermonster at the end.

Beginner's Strategy: When you start out in World of Forest, go to the right, bust the Bricks for Armor and Weapons, and drop into the first pit. Head left. Break the wall there and claim the Magic Lamp and Armor. Important: After claiming the Magic Lamp, make certain you don't pick up any other Object (that is, Ring, Poison, etc.), or the new Object will replace the lamp. Using the Iron Ball and Chain as your weapon, head to the right, slug monsters as you go, and climb the Vine back to the surface. At the end of the path (you won't be able to go further) drop down the pit. (Watch out: Just before you get here, Kat the archer will be hiding in a tree.) Stay on the bottom of level, not going up any of the Vines. When you reach the green wall on your right, go through the Bricks; the Lamp will automatically spirit you to the next world. If you're feeling brave, you can always go aboveground and fight the Killer Tree . . . though you'll be going out on a limb to do so.

If you decide you *want* to tackle the Tree, here's some advice. As you journey through this World, you will encounter red and white Mushrooms. There'll be one clump of two; pass these by, and when you reach the next Mushroom, hop on top of it and crouch down —you will automatically be armed to the gills with all of the most potent weapons the game has to offer! Continue forth until you reach the Fireball-blowing, root-waving Tree. Look at the background; you'll see the silhouettes of two trees in the distance, behind you. In rhythm with the Fireballs, move from the left edge of the screen to the right, no closer to the Killer Tree than the second tree in the background. Shoot flame from your sword all the while, and before long you'll scorch the Killer Tree to death.

In the World of Caverns, go down the first pit. Stay on the uppermost of the two levels, or you'll have to fight the tough, flaming Medusas who slither along the bottom. As you go, whack at the Bricks on the roof of the cavern. Right before the pit leading back up, the roof

Bricks will bestow the Pegasus Wings upon you, giving you the power of flight. Be careful: There are monsters waiting for you on top of the pit. Ascend, take a quick peek at where they are (and we mean *quick)*, drop back now that you know where to strike, and exit with your weapon singing! When you get back up, stay on the top level of the cavern. As you fly through, drop down to club whatever monsters pass beneath you. However, make sure you keep the Iron Ball and Chain; it's the best weapon to use against the Golem, a lumbering stone giant whose arms shoot stone projectiles and whose head disattaches and chases you. When you greet the fiend, *immediately* attack the head, before it can get you on the run or corner you. It'll pop pretty easily. Afterward, fly behind the body and stay there, where the stone projectiles can't get you. Keep hitting the Golem until it dies.

Advanced Strategy: The World of Sea is the toughest of all the realms. First of all, sad but true, even if you get through the World of Caverns unscathed, you still lose your Pegasus Wings when you reach the Sea. It'd be nice if you could fly over it! Since that isn't the case— dive in, go to the Bricks on the bottom left, and claim the Armor, Helmet, and Hammer. Go to the next set of Bricks (where the Life Flower is sprouting) and shatter the Bricks for the Iron Ball and Chain. When you swim past the first blue Pyramid, you'll come to a collection of Bricks overhead; jump up, using your helmeted noggin to smash them. Inside is the Shell Necklace, which transforms Athena into a Mermaid. Without it, you will never get through some of the narrow passages ahead. (On rare occasions the Necklace will appear on the ledge before you drop underwater. Look for it!) Continue on, positioning yourself just to the right of the halfway point in the screen, and *keep moving forward*. There will be monsters behind you; let them chase you. Don't stop and fight until the Pablos appear ahead of you. You'll have to stop then, at which point take them out, then turn and slaughter the beasts behind you. This method saves a lot of time. (Note: More than ever, avoid getting the Arrows down here. By the same token, keep your eyes open for the Scroll, which is dropped now and then.) With the Discuses, you'll have no trouble cutting your way through the Davis, Joss, and other foes you'll meet. When you finally reach the Fire Octopus, stay to the upper-left corner of its lair. The monster is on the right, and its Fireballs will arc toward you . . . but they can't reach you up there. Wait until the last of the flaming spitballs has been spat, then drop down. Rap the tentacled twit in the mouth and get away, back into the upper left corner. Repeat as often as necessary. For fun (?), you can also try to slither around behind the red scourge.

The World of Sky is next, and you'll need to get Pegasus Wings from the Bricks. Fighting the Flying Horses and Lions isn't terribly difficult: Two hits each from a Hammer will slay them. When you face the 3-headed dragon at the end, hit the heads to kill it. You'll go to the World of Ice after that, but it's neither slippery nor very different, strategy-wise, from what's gone before.

Par: You should be able to score 10,000 points per level.

Training Tips: It would be a good idea to stick around the first level, uncovering all the weapons and learning how to use them all. Sometimes when a weapon falls from a Brick, you may not be able to avoid it; in such cases, you'd darn well better know how to wield it effectively!

Rating: Although this game is reminiscent of *Karnov* in gameplay and layout, it has its own unique charm and daunting monsters. A major complaint: Except for the Medusa and Gabbys, the animation and design of the monsters is pretty pedestrian. The scenery is also boring.

Challenge: B

Graphics: C

Sound: B—

CHAPTER THREE

BIONIC COMMANDO

Type: Search-and-destroy.

Objective: Super Joe is one heck of a hero . . . and he's been captured by the Imperial Forces of the tyrant Generalissimo Killt. Enter an even greater hero, the Bionic Commando, whose job is to search through enemy territory, seeking spies (and clues), fighting Killt's Soldiers and exotic weapons, and rescuing Super Joe.

Layout: The screen scrolls horizontally and vertically. There are also overhead Bonus Screens.

Hero: Before acquiring any special weapons, the Bionic Commando has the ability to walk, crouch, shoot, and to extend his Bionic Arm. This can be used to climb, swing over precipices, or catch objects left behind by dead Soldiers. (With the rare exception of a few monsters, such as the Giant Moths, he can't use it to disarm Soldiers or automated foes . . . though by hitting them, he can bump them back a bit). On the Bonus Screens, by hitting the A button, the Commando can also swing his arm overhead, like a chopper propeller, to thwack away enemies *and* bullets! The additional weapons Joe can acquire are all described in the instruction booklet.

Enemies: The Soldiers and their destructive vehicles and automatons are outlined in the booklet. Some of the ghastly obstacles that *aren't* mentioned are discussed below.

Menu: There is only the one-player game.

Scoring: You play only for Energy (and victory!)

Beginner's Strategy: A few general pointers. One: If you ever find yourself falling off a cliff or down a pit, don't assume you're doomed. You can always fire your Bionic Arm toward a ledge or piece of machinery or whatever, catch on, and climb back up. Two: You can't go into rooms without having entered *all* the rooms before it. That holds true when you lose a life and go back to the beginning; you can't just romp back to where you died, you have to enter every room. Four: Though it may seem impossible at first, you can leap rows of Barrels or Crates. Swing up, and while you're swinging, shoot out again, diagonally, get a hold on the top of the Barrels, and you'll make it to the top. Five: You can't be shot if you're crouching. Bullets (or the electricity of Barrier Soldiers, etc.) pass right over or stop short of your head. However, if an enemy is crouched behind a barrel or obstacle, *it* can't be killed either. What you have to do is go to the other side, squat, then get up and gun them down ASAP!

One *very* important point. Ordinarily, if you lose all your lives, you can't continue the game from where you died. That's a bummer —but there's a way around it! At the beginning of the game, on the Map Screen, access the Transfer mode and move to point Four. Your Chopper will collide with an enemy Truck, and you'll be spirited right to a Bonus Screen. Fight your way along (it's easy), and make sure you shoot the Soldiers carrying the Shields. They'll leave behind Eagles; get them. Every Eagle you capture enables you to start the game over once from the level at which you died. Since Bonus Screens occur with some regularity, this means you may never have to go back to the beginning. Ever! Now, on to a tour of the first few levels.

At the end of the Bonus Screen enter the Bunker and start the game proper. You'll be back on the Map Screen: move your Chopper to point One. Climb the tower, enter the room on top, leave, continue right, and climb to the top of the second building. Enter the room and go down using the Elevator. Skip the first passages (they're blue) on the left and right. At the second pair of passages, head right and enter the door. Get the communiqué there. Go back to the center (Elevator) pass, use your arm to descend to the next horizontal passage on the left (watching out for the paratrooper). Go all the way to the left, then up to the ledge just below the next blue passage on the left.

Watch for a (beneficial!) surprise to float down here. Climb, killing Soldiers and gaining Energy. Go to the top, then head left into the passage. You'll be greeted by a deadly wall of electricity. Extend your Bionic Arm straight up and hang just under the ceiling, shooting left . . . not at the electricity, but at the generator above it. It's easily destroyed, and the electrical barrier will vanish. Go left into the door. Get on the level in the middle of the screen and head right. The Soldiers are easy to slay here: your goal is the Main System Reactor on the far right. Shoot the glowing center a few times, and the whole shebang will go up in smoke. For reaching the end of the level, you'll be rewarded with Medicine.

Back at the Map Screen, transfer to point Two. (If, in the process, you collide with an enemy Truck and find yourself in a Bonus Round, fine and dandy! Get more Eagles, natch.) Arriving in level two, you'll be rained on by paratroopers. Fight 'em off as you move to the right. Inside the room you'll face crawling pools of Ooze. These slow you down but aren't too pesky here. In fact, you can let them carry you as far as the pit on the right, which is your destination anyway! When you get there, whether by Ooze express or Bionic Arm, make sure you swing out before you fall in. Climb straight up to the ledge under the Crane Caterpillar. Wait until the malevolent mechanism starts moving to the right, then swing up, land on the same ledge it's on, face it, and blast the thing to metal filings! Ascend, destroy the Crane Caterpillar on the left as it moves to the left, then head left to the door. Exit, go left again (swinging over the next two Crane Caterpillars if you don't feel like whupping them). Beyond the second of these Caterpillars, at the pit on the left, jump down as far as the yellow ledge with a blue corridor just to its left. Enter the door there. You'll face the same end-of-level foe as you did in round one, and should win just as easily . . . even though there are a few more Soldiers. You earn a Charm here for your valiant efforts!

Go to the Map Screen and point Three. More new foes await! To begin with, there's Quicksand to the right. Swing over the first pool, keeping an eye out for a parachuting goody. When you reach the two Trees, you'll be at a pool of Quicksand you won't be able to swing over; swing as far across as you can, walk as you sink, and either keep trudging to the other side (you'll make it, even though you're slowly being swallowed up), or else use your Bionic Arm to latch onto the Tree on the other side. On the next tower you'll have some overgrown insects and carnivorous vegetation to deal with: Giant Spiders (they take a couple of shots to beat), Human-Eating Deadly Seed-Spitting Plants that burst up from rippling spots in the ground, and Giant Moths. Make your way to the right side of the tower and climb straight up. Watch for the Moths; when you see them on the right, you'll know there's a door just above, on the left. Get to it. (Be careful: There's a plant just to the left of the door, so don't overshoot it!). Enter—being aware of the fact that if you slip here, you'll land on floors and some ledges that are lined with deadly Spikes!

Ride the Elevator down to the second Elevator, then hop off it immediately, into the passage on the right. Go to the Elevator on the right, descend one level (to the first opening on the left), enter, and continue left to the next door. In this end-of-level room, you face a different kind of headache: a Cannonmobile shooting at you from the right. Get on the middle ledge again, but be prepared to dodge its artillery. The problem here is that you have to be close to the thing in order to destroy it. But a few well-placed shots in its cannon will do the trick, after which you shoot the Reactor as before, collect your Rapid Fire reward, and move on to the next level!

Advanced Strategy: Transfer to point Four, though this time you'll find that Jeeps and more Soldiers have been added to the enemy's arsenal. Get the Eagles as before . . . and get set for a dangerous but incredible level!

Almost at once you'll enter a dark cave on the right. The shadows cast by the rocks conceal shadowy soldiers; you'll have to keep a keen eye out to see these buggers! Go to the right, on the bottom, then climb up one level when you reach the far right. Enter the door, see what there is to see in there, exit, and ascend until you reach the green Grates. There are blue platforms above them; cross to the right on these. Go out the door on the upper right, though be extracautious: The soldiers in this corner of the room are stealthy and almost impossible to see! You're now in the end-of-level room; frankly, just stay out of the way of the tough-as-steel Soldier here. Just concentrate on shooting the core of the Reactor, and you'll get a Wide Gun as a reward.

Send your Chopper to point Five and, when you arrive, climb this massive—and we mean massive!—structure all the way to the top. Watch out, as you climb, for the occasional Ball and Chain, which snaps loose and rolls at you. (Once you're good at this level, have fun swinging over a Ball and Chain and kicking it to knock it around a bit.) Enter the door at the top, but be ready to deal with the Barrier Soldiers when you emerge. Their electric guns will turn you into a french fry. In order to reach these hovering bothers, use your Bionic Arm to ascend, shooting when the flying fiends are in your sight. Continue up to the next door, crouching to avoid Barrier Soldier beams, if you have no choice (better to wait than meet your Maker). About now, pay attention for a goody that will come dropping from the sky. Continue up, enter the third room of the tower, and fight another Cannonmobile to get to the Reactor. When you win this one, you earn a valuable Rocket Launcher.

Transfer to point Six and battle your way through the Bonus Screen. There are *mucho* more Soldiers here than before; the best way through is to go straight up the center, with brief trips to the side to get around barriers.

The next level is a nighttime battleground. Pods leap up at you from the pits, and be alert for the One-Up life you can obtain (it's just sitting peacefully, yoga-style, on an overhead ledge). Leap the pits, fight the robot at the end of your progress to the right, and climb. In order to proceed here, you've got some tough, precision swinging to do; you have to swing from Pole to Pole by attaching yourself to the ball on top (you can also perch on the balls, if you have to). Enter the room after the first row of Poles, then continue to the right, across two more Poles (a little and big one). Be careful not to get bopped by the red Pods here . . . and climb, Commando!

Keep in mind that you'll have an impossible time in Six unless you have the Rocket Launcher, and a worse time in Seven without the 3-Way Gun. Also remember this: When you reach the Neutral Zone (15), you'll need a gun to get through the impasse there. Even though gunfire will attract enemies like pit bulls at a barbeque, you have no choice. There's no other way to get through. You should be able to pick your way through on your own, but we do offer one final word: when you get to the last Bonus Screen, don't waste your time trying to kill the Commander. He can't be beaten. You'll simply have to think of some other way to sneak into the Bunker!

Par: Getting to the end of the fourth level is considered a tad above average.

Training Tips: Since most of us don't have Bionic

limbs, it's going to take you a while to learn how to use Joe's effectively. Start the game, and stay at the beginning of the first level until you've mastered the simple art of climbing and swinging. Make sure you can swing up and around Barrels. When this becomes second nature, you'll be able to turn the Generalissimo into hamburger. However, if all else fails, and you find yourself trapped in an area, or not sufficiently armed, there's an easy way to get out. Hold down the Start button, the A button, and the B button at the same time. This will transport you to safety!

Rating: This is a super-fun game of the *Contra* school, with the terrific gameplay element of Joe's extendible arm. Note: The only drawback is that the instruction booklet was written by someone with the literacy level of toast. (Of the Wide Gun, it says, "You can shoot at wide range but reach is shoot." Come again? Or did they mean to say, "reach is *short*"?) See our not-too-happy comments about this problem in the Rating section for ZANAC.

Challenge: A

Graphics: B+

Sound: B− (they could have come up with some imaginative Bionic Arm sound.)

CHAPTER FOUR

BLASTER MASTER

Type: Seek-and-destroy quest.

Objective: Jason and his frog Fred are pals. Alas, when Fred stumbles onto a leaking box of plutonium, he mutates . . . and leaps down a hole to an underground realm of mutants. Boldly, Jason pursues his pet, hoping to destroy the Mutant Plutonium Warlord who rules the monsters.

Layout: The screen scrolls vertically and horizontally, depending upon the level. There are eight Stages in the game.

Hero: Jason comes equipped with a Gun and an armored, leaping Rover. He has the ability to leave the vehicle and go exploring. Along the way, Jason acquires Power Pills and other abilities and weapons, which are described in the instruction booklet (many are also discussed below, in Beginner's Strategy).

Enemies: Mutants of all shapes and sizes, most notably the lesser Warlords that rule each level. More in the instruction booklet, and see

below. Also watch out for the lethal Plutonium rocks, Turrets (like the one you'll encounter in the second vertical level of Stage
One), Keys to open locked doors, and the like.

Menu: There's only the one-player quest.

Scoring: Jason and the Rover earn (and lose)
powers as they go.

Beginner's Strategy: *Blaster Master* is an extremely complex game, with more rooms
than the Empire State Building! What's more,
many of them are hidden (see Advanced
Strategy). To keep this write-up from becoming as sprawling as the Mutant hive itself,
we're going to give you an overview of the first
Stage and general tips to the rest. That will be
enough to get you going and well into the
game!

As you enter Stage One you'll need to hop
down two ledges to the Door. (Keep in mind
that if you avoid the door and continue to the
bottom of this vertical screen, you'll end up at
the Door to Stage Four. File this information;
you'll need to get back here later! Going
through the Stage One Door, you must cross
from ledge to ledge and cliff to cliff until you
reach the Door on the far right. Descend four
ledges to the next door and enter the subterra-
nean forest. Go right, then down the Ladder to
the Door. You'll find two rooms down here,
with weapons at the top right of the upper
room; look for a Hover Capsule, Thunder
Break, Multi-Warhead Missile, and/or Gun
Capsule. You'll have to blast the wall to get
them; also, obviously, time your run to the

rear wall so that the orbiting bombs of the Mutant here don't clobber you. Leave and go back up the Ladder. Continue to the right and go down the pit (a total of eight ledges). There are several weapons caches you can get to from here; choose as many as you like. These are:

A. Enter the deepest labyrinth (the watery cavery below you), take Staircase One to the left, swim right a short distance (descending as you go), then take the left-pointing Staircase Two. Head left; at the end of this corridor is a four-room region containing more powers.

B. Instead of going into the blue, go to the right. Climb the platforms ahead, cross the plateau, jump up the ledges until you reach the forest again, head left, leap the first pit and go down the second; there's a door on a ledge halfway down. Inside, in the upper-right corner of the top room, are more powers.

C. After clearing out B, there's another chamber down and to the left. You can't just drive down, however; you'll have to think about this one!

D. The final weapons warehouse is way to the bottom right. Instead of heading to the surface at the plateau mentioned in B, continue to the right. Descend and go back into the water. Head down and right to the very bottom, then travel due right until you come to the Ladder. Ascend, and you'll find a

three-room stronghold with many Power
Capsules.

To get to Stage Two, go to that eighth ledge,
which led to the water world. Hop to the left
(over the water), and continue in that direction until you reach a door. Go through it,
then down the ledges to the bottom of the vertical screen. Use your Gun to defeat the mutant Brain and its detachable Cells, and you
can enter Stage Two using Hyper.

Advanced Strategy: You'll find yourself in a horizontal cavern; cross to the right, leaping three
pits. You will find yourself, now, at the bottom
of a towering vertical pit. As you ascend keep
this in mind: Things aren't always what they
seem! You may run into a wall in your travels
and have to backtrack; if you return to that
spot later, it may not be what it was before!

In successive Stages make sure you have obtained the following powers from Stage
Bosses in order to continue: Hover (at Three),
Keys (Four), Diving (Five), Wall-1 (wall-walk-
ing power; Six), and Wall-2 (ceiling-walking
ability; Seven). Be aware, though, that the
Stages can't be reached directly in numerical
order: One leads to Two and Four; Four leads
to Five; Five gets you to Six; Seven and Three
can only be reached from Two; and you won't
get to Eight any way but by passing through
Three. And don't try to take them out of order:
for instance, you won't get far in Stage Seven
unless you've first conquered Six and obtained
Wall-1!

A general rule about battling the Stage Bosses: Don't stand still! Each Mutant will be firing things at you, and at the same time you should be moving and shooting back, looking for its particular weak spots.

Here's a special tip: When you come to Stage Five at the end of Four, there are two Doors, and you need a Key for each. If you only have the one you got for killing the long-tongued, fireball-spitting Frog Mutant at the climax of Stage Four, don't despair! Open the first Door, drive in, get out of the ol' Rover, and climb the Ladder all the way up. Take a mighty leap from the top, staying close to the wall on the right; if you land on the lock, you'll open the Door. You'll lose that Jason's life . . . but it's better than standing around with your hands in your pockets, unable to continue!

Without a doubt, the toughest foe you'll face in the game is the mutant frog in Stage Four. However, there's one sure way to send it to toad heaven. When it sticks out its tongue, get to the left of the mouth, just about level with its leg. Shoot at the mouth, move to avoid the fireballs, then shoot again. Those early shots you got in will have weakened the monster considerably, so beating it will be a cinch. At least, it'll be cinchier than if you had just been running around, shooting wild.

Of course, the other bosses aren't a piece of cake either, but here's a tip to help you destroy them. Hit the Start button as soon as you've fired a Grenade. That will pause the action . . . but not the Grenade. It'll keep on working. Thus, when you de-activate the pause mode, your foe will usually be dead.

Par: This is a tough game. An average player should be able to get through most of two levels.

Training Tips: Your vehicle and Jason are fairly tough and versatile, so the best thing you can do for yourself is make your own detailed map of the Mutant world. That's really what you're going to need to get through! It's also a good idea to completely master the art of getting in and out of the Rover in a hurry. You'll be doing a lot of this as you proceed.

Rating: This cartridge is very difficult, and it's a lot of fun to map . . . with some pretty wiggy, tough-to-kill monsters.

Challenge: A—
Graphics: B+
Sound: B—

CHAPTER FIVE

BOMBERMAN

Type: Pursuit through a maze.

Objective: Betcha didn't know that even robots can get bored. It's true, and Bomberman is an automaton totally fed up with life in the bomb-manufacturing factory. Learning that it's possible to escape from the plant, and to become human when you reach the surface, he sets out on the perilous journey. Exitways are hidden beneath Bricks, which must be exploded; Bomberman can only pass through one, to the next room, when all the monsters have been cleared from the screen.

Layout: Each room is roughly twice as long as your TV screen; the screen scrolls horizontally as Bomberman picks his way through the peril-filled mazes. Every room has a different configuration, and monsters and Power-Up Symbols are found in the different places from screen to screen (even on the same level).

Hero: When he sets out, Bomberman can move

in any direction and has the power to set Bombs, whose explosions destroy Bricks (though not Concrete) and reach two Brick lengths down an open corridor. He can only put down one Bomb at a time; only when it explodes can he lay down another. He can acquire other powers as he goes along: these are located in Power-Up Symbols underneath Bricks, and include the ability to put down more than one Bomb at a time (though you won't want to deposit more than 6 in a line, since you won't be able to duck away from the blast before the first Bomb explodes); the power to walk through Bricks (including Concrete); invulnerability (inside the "?", though it only lasts as long as the music lasts); Bombs that blast farther; and the very valuable detonate-at-will power, which allows you to cause the Bombs to explode when you wish them to. By the way, when you lose a life, you lose all Power-Ups (except for any multiple-Bomb powers you've acquired by reaching certain plateaus in the game). Note: Individual Bomb explosions reach farther when they're set off side by side.

Enemies: There are eight different foes, all of them pictured in the booklet. Their abilities (not described there) are as follows: Valcom moves slowly and does not run from you or Bombs; O'Neal is slightly faster; Dahl moves only horizontally or vertically, never both; Minvo first appears on level four, will lie in wait to pounce on you, and is the first monster you'll meet that can overtake you; Ovape moves *through* any Brick or Concrete, will sometimes sniff you out in a nook, isn't very fleet, but is smart enough to turn, and moves away from Bombs (the best way to kill 'em is to lure them to a corner and drop Bombs along their escape routes); Doria has the same power as Ovape but is very slow in reacting to a Bomb and is easier to kill (it will die if you blow up a Brick that it's more than half covering); Pass is very fast (and doesn't arrive until the fourteenth level); and Pontan, which arrives only when the clock has run down and you still haven't cleared a level, is skinny, fast, comes at you in vast numbers, and is murder to murder!

All of the monsters follow you as you move, though Ovape tends to drift toward the Exitway once it's been exposed (meaning that if you try to blast it there, you may blast the Exitway and release more monsters). An important note about the monsters: Even if they're off screen, even if you haven't seen them as yet, if a monster is in the way of a blast, it will perish. There's little that's more gratifying in this game than to move ahead in the wake of an explosion and see that you've killed a creature you didn't even know was there! Also, even if a monster runs into the flame of a blast after the Bomb has exploded, it will perish. Finally, a horde of monsters not only appears if you accidentally blow up an Exitway, but also if you blow up a Power-Up Symbol.

Menu: There is just the one-player game.

Scoring: Bomberman earns points for slaying

foes (from 100 to 8000); this includes the monsters that you release when you detonate a Bomb too close to an Exitway. There is also a bonus round every fifth screen. Bomberman races against a 200-second clock.

Beginner's Strategy: In the early screens (through fourteen or so), a good strategy is to move about the left side of the screen (which is where you begin), blasting Bricks in search of the Exitway; it's usually on this side in all rounds. Finding it, move to the right side and destroy the monsters there. Then go back to the Exitway side; it's best to be near there, obviously, as the clock runs down!

When you have a low number of monsters to deal with, a good strategy is to force them into a corner gradually; lay a Bomb between you and the monster, get out of range (so will the monster), run ahead when it explodes, drop another Bomb closer to the corner, retreat, and so on, until you've got your enemy's back to the wall. Obviously, this will only work along a corridor top, bottom, or sides . . . so don't go blowing up all the Bricks willy-nilly. You'll need some of them! As a rule, once you have two-Bomb capacity or more, you should start trying to hem monsters in. On screens where you have to free monsters from Brick cages (such as Minvo), put down the Bomb to open the cage and, if there's only one way out, place a Bomb a Brick or two farther away. The first one will detonate and the monster will escape . . . running smack-dab into the second when it blows! Naturally, put down the first Bomb, if possible, so that the monster has to travel down a long corridor. This will give the beastie less time to escape into another passage before the fireworks begin! (Note: Since Bombs erupt in four directions, make sure, when you lay one down, that you're not freeing a monster you wanted to keep captive a little longer!)

Be careful not to make a few common mistakes. Don't box yourself in between a creature and a dead end (in haste, many people set down a Bomb to kill a creature before noticing that they, themselves, have no way out!). Don't set two Bombs to kill a monster and impulsively move out if you've been lucky enough to destroy the monster with the first—thus walking into the explosion from the second and dying. And don't go plopping down Bombs so that they overlap. If you do this and expose the Exitway with an early Bomb, one of the subsequent explosions may open it, releasing monsters. (Some players prefer to leave the finding of the Exitway for last. However, this wastes a lot of time. You should blast Bricks when you pass them, so that you don't have to race back and do it later, when all the monsters are dead.)

Here are a couple of passwords to bring you right to various levels:

Three: FEPCOBFEFHOLOLKEFEFH
Seven: FEBABAMNMADJDJOMNMNH
Eleven: ABMNDDNMNNABABPJDJDL
Thirteen: JDBABAMIHFNMNMPPCPCH

Advanced Strategy: On later screens, when there are more and more Bricks (starting with room twenty-two), you'll be blocked into a small area on top. Shoot paths along the top and left side, then make your way to the vertical center of the screen and chew holes horizontally through the Bricks. It's important to have a long horizontal passage; if you lay down 5 or 6 Bombs one after the other, then duck out of the way, you can nail more monsters (especially the pesky Ovapes) than you would if you hunted them down.

Note: Watch out for level twenty-one! It has Dorias and Ovapes both . . . the two kinds of critter that can pass through Bricks!

Here are a few passwords that will whisk you to some of the later screens:

Fourteen: JDHIMECGKFNMNMPPCPCN

Seventeen: FEKGDANDJLLOLOIJDDJL

Twenty: NMFEMODIHHLOLOOBAHIG

Twenty-seven:

DJLOEHCMNNCPCPDJDDJC

Thirty-four: DJIHPPBLOGJDJDPDJIHC (a toughie, since there's a solid layer of Brick across the top).

Par: Points vary dramatically, since many more experienced players like to blast Exitways to release monsters for points. In general, you should be able to clear rooms one through twelve in 80 seconds, fourteen through twenty in 100, and beyond that in 120 seconds.

Training Tips: The best way to polish your skills is to go to one of the rooms in the twenties, find the door at once, Bomb it a few times—releas-

ing a horde of monsters—and just try to survive . . . let alone destroy creatures!

Rating: Although the rooms and monsters aren't
all that much different, and the game has a
sameness to it after a while, it offers the same
addictive fun as *Pac-Man, Dig-Dug,* and similar maze-type games. Two complaints, albeit
minor ones: The passwords are a real pain to
input; and because of the random way the
mazes and monsters are generated, a later
stage will occasionally begin with you
hemmed into a tiny area . . . and a monster
right beside you. You die even before you can
set a Bomb!

Challenge: B+

Graphics: B+ (awe-inspiring explosions . . .
especially 6 side by side)

Sound: B−

CHAPTER SIX

CITY CONNECTION

Type: Race-and-shoot.

Objective: You've robbed a paint store, and your car's leaking paint. But that's not the worst of it. The Police (and other traffic) are out in force! Unfortunately, you can't leave a given City for the next until you've spread paint over every inch of the three levels of Highway in the metropolis!

Layout: The screen scrolls horizontally. There are six Cities in all. Though the arrangement of the Highways is always the same, the appearance of Cats, Oil Cans, and Roadblocks is random.

Hero: Your getaway Car has the ability to race, jump up or down, brake and turn, or fire Oil Cans to dispose of vehicles that are in your way. A skillful player will be able to jump off a Highway, turn in midair, and get onto the Highway directly underneath! Balloons appear at random; collecting three of these will spirit you to another City. (See instruction booklet for special tips on Balloons. Incidentally, when you get the 3 balloons, the warp-ahead, super-speed graphics are a knockout . . . *and* you get showered with points!). Balloons usually track with you, and will stay on the screen as long as you don't race away and cause them to scroll off. You get extra Cars in your stockpile at various point plateaus (see instructions).

Enemies: In addition to the various Cars, Cats appear. On the lowest level of any Highway system, these tend to appear in twos, bracketing you in. However, if you leave a screen and double back, the Cat that had appeared will usually be gone. Ditto the Road Blocks that grow from the pavement when you've spent too long on that level. Plus: They, too, can be jumped, though it's a *really* tight squeeze if you're under a tier! The Highways are likewise your enemies. And as you proceed in the game, you'll notice that their positions are such so that it's difficult to hop cleanly from one to the other. You'll really have to make a lot of worming jumps to shift levels.

Menu: Two players can enjoy the game on alternating turns.

Scoring: You earn points for Oil Cans, for hitting Cars, and for painting the City white in as few miles as possible.

Beginner's Strategy: This can't be stressed enough: Regardless of what City you're in, work your way from the top to the bottom. (It helps that if you lose a car, you always start again on the top of the screen; at least you don't have to make your way back to the top.) This isn't to say you should stay just on the top level to start; hop between the upper and middle until they're both coated. Try and save the bottom tier for last. If you do end up down there before the top two rows of Highway are finished, get off it quickly.

The best thing to do is race along the top level until you've coated all or most of every section of Highway up there. So as not to remain on the level too long (and bring on the Roadblock) drop down and take the next tier after one complete pass above. More than likely, the very edges of the upper section of Highway will be unpainted. When you've had a good, solid run across the tier below, hop back up, dab any unpainted edges, then drop back down. Although you're awarded points for Oil Cans, and can certainly use them during the game, don't go out of your way to grab them! Painting must be your first priority. When you have to go racing along the bottom, it's a good idea to fire ahead, to stop any Cars (being ready to brake for Cats, of course). Also, if you see a Car on an upper tier and it's pacing you, you might want to slow just a bit, fire an Oil Can when the other Car is about to drop down, and thus have your shot intercept it.

In the first City, New York, it's possible to use a "sewing" method to finish off unpainted edges on different tiers one directly atop the other. Starting at the top, paint the edge there, drop off, and turn back—twisting and doubling back in midair.

Advanced Strategy: Key maneuvers always to keep in mind, and typical blunders, are as follows: Don't drop off a tier onto a Car below; don't jump up when a Car is slightly behind you overhead, or you'll most likely collide between tiers; and if you need to jump up in one of the later Cities, start your run while you're beneath the midpoint of a tier—you'll need that much runway in order to get up! Also, if you want to get the very edge of a tier with some fancy finger work, simply tap the controller or joystick from side to side quickly, and you'll proceed by stops and starts. This will enable you to coat the tiniest portions of edge without falling off. Lastly, one thing to avoid is changing directions when you fire an Oil Can. You will automatically shoot two— one in each direction!

You'll have to have good eyesight when you reach Frankfurt (the fourth City), as the Highways are a pale gray. It's tough to tell when they've been painted! And when you hit New Delhi (City five), you'll discover that you can no longer remain on one tier simply by hopping from Highway section to section; the gaps are too large. You will constantly be changing tiers (and crying tears).

Par: You should be able to cover each City with roughly 1000 miles of travel earning 35,000 points. A decent player will complete three Cities without much problem.

Training Tips: Race without shooting. Cars aren't

your problem, the rotten Cat is! If you can jump with finesse, then the Cat won't be a problem. Think of how far you'll go when you put the deadly Oil Cans back into your bag of tricks!

Rating: A wholly original, thoroughly enjoyable, very challenging cartridge with some incredible city panoramas and considerable attention to gameplay detail (note how the [sadistic!] game designers made the river in London look a great deal like a tier of Highway . . . just to give you grief!).

Challenge: A
Graphics: A
Sound: C

CHAPTER SEVEN

DOUBLE DRAGON

Type: Martial-arts competition.

Objective: You're martial-arts expert Billy, and your beloved girlfriend Marian has been abducted by a ruthless gang known as the Black Warriors. Using your awesome skills, you must crack skulls and traverse many parts of the city (each one being described as a "Mission") in order to save her.

Layout: The screen scrolls horizontally.

Hero: Billy begins the match with the ability to Kick and Punch. As he scores victories, he acquires other abilities, such as the Jump Kick (see details, below). You can also pick up and use the various weapons dropped by defeated foes (Oil Drums, Knives, and others discussed below).

Enemies: Your foes come with a variety of skill levels and weapons. These are discussed in the two Strategy entries. Note: Don't back away just because baddies are down. They

may well get up again! Your enemies all
flicker before they die.

Menu: One- or two-player games can enjoy alter-
nate games. The cartridge also offers a mode
in which two players can fight each other
without the presence of the Warriors.

Scoring: Billy earns points for introducing enemies to his feet, knee, and the bottom of his
shoe.

Beginner's Strategy: Your enemies always attack
from the same place, in the same numbers. At
the beginning of Mission One use your Kick
against the first attackers. Climb the Ladder
on the right, go right, wait by the second Ladder, and Kick your enemies in the head as
they climb up. Go down and finish them off.
Continue right, Kicking foes. When Lopar the
Oil Drum-bearer arrives, back away so you
won't get hit, pick it up, and use it as a
weapon. (If you're good, you can run up to the
Drum, press A, hoist it, and chuck it at the
hostile dude.) Go all the way to the right, to
the wall, and fight the attackers who come
from the left. Enter the door. In the Conveyor
Belt Boss Room move to the top of the screen,
off the Belt, and thus lure your enemies there.
Get to the left of them and knock them right,
off the ledge. When Abobo arrives, stay on the
Conveyor Belt, to the left, and bash him to the
right, off the edge.

To help you through Mission Two, you will
earn a new power hereabout: the Uppercut.
It'll take you four or five hits to knock your
first foes down . . . and then they'll just get

up again, so you have to repeat. Next up is wicked Williams and his Dynamite. Don't be afraid, though—you can use it against him. Wait until he throws it, then move back. Williams will follow you. Stop moving when he's right on top of his own sizzling explosive; when it blows, the Warriors'll need tweezers to collect their comrade-in-arms. Go right, climb the Fence, and jump over your foe Williams to avoid his Bat. While he's still facing the other way, Kick him in the back of the head. Pick up the Bat and beat his brains out.

At this point, if you wish to "cheat," there's another strategy you can employ. Get the Bat, climb from the Fence, and head right. Watch for the final member of an attacking trio—Williams, who will be packing Dynamite. Move up on the screen, to the middle of the stacked Girders, until the bottom of your feet are level with the bottom of the Girders. The Dynamiter will come after you. Scoot around him and reclimb the Fence before your foe—who will come after you—reaches the end of the Girders. Climb; Williams will be paralyzed! Move as far left as you can, climb down, and go back to where you last saw Williams. He'll be gone. However, using the Bat or Kicking in that spot will earn you oodles of points, and, if you're lucky, all seven additional powers!

If you don't want to use this strategy, when the three enemies appear, beat up the first one, then wait until the Dynamite is tossed and deal with it as before. This time, though, the remaining two enemies will stick close together; there's an excellent chance the explosive will destroy them both! You'll be rewarded with the ultraessential Jump Kick about this time. Go right, climb the Ladder, fight the Whip-wielding Linda who comes from the left, take the Whip, and continue up the second Ladder (watching for a Linda who is usually climbing down about now). Lash her, go up the third and fourth Ladders, and when you face the mighty Chintai, use Uppercuts and Jump Kicks to best him. It takes a lot to whip this Warrior, but stick with it. (If you can't be bothered fighting, here's all you do: When Chintai shows up, go back down the Ladder. You will be transported right to Mission Three!)

Advanced Strategy: You're ready for Mission Three now—a seemingly pastoral forest. But beware! A Warrior will arrive and fling a Knife at you. Stay far away so you can dodge it, then clobber the would-be killer. (If you're good *and* fast, slink in and Jump Kick the creep before he can throw it. You can pick up the Knife and use it!) A pair of Chintais are up next, one leaping at you from atop a tree, another running at you with a Knife. You have enough time, though, to take out the first before the second arrives. Deal with the Knife tosser as before. You've got another gruesome twosome to deal with next; one tough nut arrives, followed within moments by a second. If you haven't beaten up the first before number two arrives, stay between them, Jump

Kicking left and right until they die. You'll get the Hair-Pull Kick about now—a terrific maneuver! (You grab a fistful of hair, pull their forehead repeatedly against your knee, then toss them over your shoulder!) Use this against your next foes. When you reach the Bridge, beat up Williams and his Bat, then have a look ahead. You'll notice the span's busted in the middle; adding to your troubles, a Warrior with a Knife is waiting on the other side. Here's what you do to get over. Go to the top of the bridge, Jump Kick to get over . . . then quickly move to the bottom on the other side. The Knife will have been thrown while you were on the top, and if you dart down quickly, it'll miss you. Punish the rat for throwing it. As you move right, stay in the exact center of the screen; it's the best place from which to launch an attack against the second Knife thrower who will appear. *Now* you get into some serious trouble. The wall ahead of you will erupt and a pair of Abobos will stalk out. Use your Jump Kick both to hurt and get over them. Your priority should be *not* to get between them, or they'll close in on you and grind you to a pulp. Rather, try leaping them and staying on the left and right of the screen to keep *them* centered. If you keep up a relentless Jump Kick attack with the two of them huddled in the middle of the screen, you will defeat them. You'll be rewarded with a fifth power here.

The next battle scene is the Cave from which the Abobos emerged. Proceed slowly, and time your steps to avoid the Stalactites that will fall from above. Ditto the Elevators up ahead; there's no strategy here other than to land on them squarely, and not fall into the pit! After clearing this section, go right and you'll face two Chintais. After fighting them, enter the cave. (Go right and you'll have to face Abobo. Don't, and you won't!) You'll dodge falling rocks, leap pits, and fight a few foes . . . but it's nothing you can't handle.

The two keys to winning Mission Four are as follows: When you're fighting Williams on the Ladders, *don't* slay him; if he lives, his Williams kin won't appear. Also, stay away from Abobo at the end. When he bursts onto the screen, climb the wall to the left and flee! Of course, that's not all it takes to win here, so here are some other tips. As this mission begins, Blocks will come sliding from the wall, trying to whack you down. You can pass them by waiting for the nearest Block to slide out twice. When it does, hurry to the right. None of the other blocks will hit you. For the struggle with Williams, here's a great way to get a secret weapon. When you face the Chintais, use a drop kick to beat them. See the knife? Wait until the last of the Chintais blinks for the fourth time, then go and get the blade. It will be transformed into a club. When you face the Lindas, bop them with the club. However, just before the fight ends, allow one of them to disarm you. Finish the fight, and when the last of the Lindas blinks for the fourth time, pick up the club. It'll transform once again, into a weapon you can use to defeat your toughest foe!

At game's end, equipped with seven new powers, you will face the Shadow Boss . . . who is none other than Billy's rotten brother Jimmy, who is every bit as skilled as his sibling. Only a superior player will beat the evil kidnaper!

Par: As a rule of thumb, you should be earning double the amount of points you tallied on the previous Mission: 5000 for the first, 10,000 the second (for a total of 15,000), 20,000 the third (for a total of 35,000), and so on.

Training Tips: When you're alone, go to the two-player combat screen and practice moves against your defenseless opponent. This will enable you to master the moves of your Billy.

Rating: This is a much better game than *Kung Fu* or any of the other martial arts challenges. Just one complaint: the terrain's pretty simple. A few more tunnels or caverns or mazes would have made this just about perfect!

Challenge: A—

Graphics: B

Sound: B—

CHAPTER EIGHT

GAUNTLET
(A TENGEN GAME)
(Gauntlet is not designed, manufactured,
sponsored or endorsed by Nintendo®)

Type: Fantasy quest and shoot-'em-up.

Objective: Morak, the Evil One, has secreted the
Sacred Orb within the walls of his stronghold,
the Gauntlet. Lacking it, the good people of
Rendar can't protect themselves against the
sadistic plunderer. However, four warriors
dare to pit their skills against Morak and his
minions. Their fate—and that of Rendar—is
in your hands.

Layout: The view is from overhead, and the
screen scrolls in all directions as you scout
from level to level. There are 100 rooms, for-
ests, "?s," etc., in the game. Objects and foes
are always in the same place from game to
game.

Hero: You can be one of four heroes, each of
whom has their own special abilities. Thyra
the Valkyrie is the most invulnerable, Thor
the Warrior is the strongest, Merlin the Wiz-
ard has Magic, and Questor the Elf is fleetest.
Each has the ability to gather eighteen items

which boost either their attack or defense strength. These are detailed in the instruction booklet; some are discussed below. Be careful: You can destroy and thus lose Potions that are in your line of fire.

Enemies: The eleven varieties of foe you'll meet in the levels are described in the instruction booklet. Note: Though the booklet states that your shots have no effect on Death, that isn't true of the Bomb Potion, which can kill even the grim reaper. Also, remember this: In many rooms (for example, number forty-five) one or more Deaths may be hanging around . . . but in a part of the maze where they can't get to you! If you don't open a wall there, you will be safe from them.

Menu: One or two players can enjoy the game simultaneously. In a two-player game, participants can join forces or—and this is cool!—they can compete against one another!

Scoring: Your hero races against dwindling energy in each numbered room and against the clock in each non-numbered chamber (100 seconds in each "?" room, 30 in every Treasure Room). As the hero runs about, he or she tries to gather energy, added strength, or invulnerability.

Beginner's Strategy: The best strategies anyone can offer are how to get through each level and what to look out for. Herewith is a brief map of several levels in the first half of the game. Note: Look for the Blocks with nicks in them (as in level Eight). These are sections of wall that you can destroy and use as a short-cut through the maze.

Level One: If you want to hop ahead a few levels, go to the top right and shoot down at the Block there; it'll open an Exit that will take you straight to Five. Fourteen: there are two Exits in this room; go to the one on the left, since it'll bring you closer to the "?" room. Fifteen: Go straight to the right to get the Flashing Tile in the bottom, then head to the upper left for a Key and go to the upper right for the Exit. You'll find yourself in a "?" room; there's some magic for you here! (By the way, you should be able to clear this room in 70 seconds.) When you hit Twenty-two, get the Potion in the lower right. In Twenty-five, stay away from the left-side Exit; it drops you to a lower level. Use the one on the upper right, which will spirit you to a "?" room. There, under a brick, is Extra Armor Potion. In Twenty-seven there are five Exits in the lower right; the third Exit from the left will take you to a Treasure Room. In Thirty the lower-left Exit leads to Thirty-one, where the Acid Puddles become annoying—so don't let yourself become cornered! The Exit in the lower right of Thirty-one will take you up to Thirty-five. (If you want to try Thirty-four, a door in the forest of Thirty-five will lead you back. And you may well want to go there, since the upper left Exit of Thirty-four leads to a Treasure Room!

Advanced Strategy: Want an unfair (but terrific) advantage to tackle later rounds? Select a two-player game, using the same characters.

Punch in the same password for each, and you'll have two equally-powered heroes. Then allow the extra hero to die and gather everything they've left behind. This allows you to double your abilities! Now then—on with the odyssey!

In Thirty-seven the Sorcerers plague you . . . a problem compounded by the fact that the Exit is hidden! Look for it within a huge clump of Trees near the top; blast the foliage, and the Exit will appear. In Thirty-eight there's a Key to the right. Exit near the middle to get to Thirty-nine. There, in the lower left (not far from the Exit), you can obtain Extra Speed Potion. In Forty there's a Key in the center and the Exit is lower right. Forty-two offers a huge maze, with the Exit in the middle, at the bottom; this Exit elevates you to level Forty-five. There, you've got a dilemma: If you touch the Trap Wall Tiles, you'll release an army of Deaths. But if you don't, the maze'll have you trapped. So . . . do it, but your best bet is to race to the door on the lower left. This will bring you to Forty-four, where it's a good idea to have a Bomb in hand for the Acid Puddles. A Treasure Room follows, the Exit of which—right side, center—will take you to Forty-nine.

You should have the hang of it by now, but here are a few additional quick tips about levels: in Fifty-one Exit bottom right to Fifty-three. There, Exit top, center. In Fifty-four you'll need a Key or you won't get out. In Fifty-seven the center Exit leads to Sixty . . .

which you'll need a Key to escape! And so it goes, right down to your final confrontation with Morak and (hopefully) your reclaiming of the Orb. Personal experience has suggested that Questor is the best-equipped of all the warriors to make the dangerous journey . . . but, obviously, you'll have to try all four characters to find the one with which you're most comfortable!

Par: The first nine levels are super-easy (Death usually doesn't appear until ten); the so-so player will have no trouble getting to Thirty-seven, when the Sorcerers start to nag you. A good player won't get into trouble until the late fifties or early sixties, when the mazes and foes become tougher and Keys are essential.

Training Tips: Obviously, in addition to shooting skills which you'll develop as you play, it would be a good idea to map every room. Since you get codes at the end of each room, it doesn't matter if you die here, as long as you learn where the weapons and Exits are and where each Exit leads. Take special care to note where the Exits are in the Treasure Rooms, so you can get the greatest amount of coins in your 30 seconds. A good way to work out the kinks in your hero is to jump right to advanced levels. Here are some useful codes: PPH M3C P3I (Questor, level Twenty), PHP BSW 963 (Questor, Thirty-five), NRF TTU NR7 (Thyra, Forty-two), BC3 SY9 ISS (Thor, Forty-two), UTL D5T LGT (Merlin, Forty-two), PPP WW3 Z30 (Questor, Treasure Room

after Forty), PHH S9Y Z60 (Questor, Fifty-six),
BMS W69 OBE (Thor, Fifty-six), and NNN
5T5 FLK (Thyra, Fifty-six). A word of warning: Many magazines and even well-meaning
friends who provide you with passwords for
Gauntlet frequently confuse the S and 5 as
well as the 1 and I symbols on screen. If a code
you've been given doesn't work, make sure
someone didn't mix these up somewhere!

Rating: This game combines the best qualities of
a shoot-'em-up cartridge with those of a quest
game. And it's faster-moving than just about
any adventure on the market! The colors and
animation are superb, and the musical score,
with its harpsichordlike sounds, is a knockout.

Challenge: A
Graphics: A
Sound: A

CHAPTER NINE

GHOSTBUSTERS

Type: Driving and shooting game (though not at the same time).

Objective: As new-to-the-business Ghostbusters, you must catch ghosts to earn money, buy better equipment, and prepare yourself for the ultimate showdown with Zuul and her minions.

Layout: There are four kinds of screens. The first is the City Map Scene, an overview of the city showing all of the Ghost-infested buildings. By moving the No-Ghosts symbol to specific buildings, you direct your Ghostbusters there. Next, there's the Road Scene, an overhead view of the freeway as you drive to the building. Then there's a Shop Scene, which shows you the goods you can buy. Next up is the Building Scene, which shows the facade of the edifice needing exorcism (two Ghostbusters stand in the street with weapons and try to capture the Ghosts). Finally, there's the Stairway Scene, the inside of Zuul's building.

Hero: Your Ghostbusters have nothing but the Ectomobile and ten grand in the bank to begin with. They earn money by nabbing ghosts, and can also run over Gas Tanks in the Road Scene (this saves you money when you have to tank up, and also time; if you run out of gas, the Ghostbusters have to get out and push the Ectomobile to the nearest station). The tools you can buy at the Shop are described in the instruction booklet, and most are discussed below. Note: In the Building Scenes you have only 15 seconds to grab Ghosts and stash them in the Trap. Otherwise, they vanish.

Enemies: Ghosts. Lots of them. (In the Road Scene they're called Roamers.) However, only in Zuul's building do they hurt you; a few taps, and you're dead. Game over. No continuation. On the road you lose money everytime you hit or are hit by another car.

Menu: One or two players can partake in the same game, each one operating a Ghostbuster in the Building Scenes.

Scoring: You usually earn $800 per Roamer, though two in a row gets you $1600 for the second. In facade scenes you earn 200 smackers per Ghost; however, if you nab more than one at the same time, the price doubles ($400 for the second, $800 for the next, and finally $1600 for the fourth). On the debit side, collisions cost you from $200 to $1000.

Beginner's Strategy: First, some statistics for the Road Scene. Sixty percent of the time, a Ghost appears with or immediately after a car. And most of these tend to be on the left side of the road. Cans of Gas usually show up every 100 miles.

To get the easy part out of the way first: On the Road Scene, stay at the bottom of the screen; when cars emerge from the top, speed up and swing ahead of them. If you play higher than that, you run the risk of many collisions; they're almost certain if you ride more than halfway up the screen.

At the beginning of the game head to the Shop and purchase the following items: a Ghost Vacuum, three Capture Traps, and a Ghost Alarm. Some players (and the instructions!) suggest you buy the Capture Beam instead of the Alarm, but we say phooey. The Vacuum is enough . . . and with Ghosts constantly descending on Zuul's abode (bringing the world ever closer to disaster), you'd better not waste time running around the city blindly without an Alarm.

Another piece of advice: Whenever you return to the map scene, run over the four Ghosts that are headed toward Zuul's building. Touching them will freeze them and slow the mustering of the Ghosts, thus enabling you to earn more money and buy some all-important gear.

Advanced Strategy: There are three things you're going to need to add to your arsenal to battle Zuul: the Anti-Ghost Suit (you can take 9 hits from Ghosts instead of a mere 3), the Hyper Beam (most useful against Gozer, at the top of the stairs), and Ghost Food (2 helpings). Trade in the Alarm and 2 Traps to make room.

When you go to the Stairway Scene, proceed up the steps with a stop-and-start motion; in other words, go ahead—the Ghosts will head toward you—stop . . . give them a moment to lose your scent . . . then continue . . . stop again . . . and so on. If things become really wicked, with bunches of Ghosts pawing at you, use the Food.

Make sure that as you ascend you open the doors to every floor. . . .

A final tip. If you want to begin the game with nearly $2 million, enter AA during the initial stage, and then put in the number 1173468723. Push the A button and you'll be rich!

Par: The average player will be able to get up the twenty-two floors of Zuul's headquarters.

Training Tips: Get plenty of sleep. You'll need it to keep your eyes open.

Rating: Frankly, I don't see the point. Most of the game is busywork, as you meander around collecting Ghosts, earning bucks, emptying your Traps, shlepping to the Shop (the Road Scene offers zippo challenge), and finally having some fun in Zuul's building. In short, the bulk of the game is drudgery city. It's amazing to think back to the early days of videogames (and the stewardship of boss James Levy) when the name Activision on a game assured you of a winner!

Challenge: D+

Graphics: B— (largely on the strength of the terrific animation of the Marshmallow Man)

Sound: B+ (there's a nifty recreation of the *Ghostbusters* theme)

CHAPTER TEN

GUN·SMOKE

Type: Western shoot-'em-up.

Objective: Billie Bob enforces the law in the wild west. While searching for the desperado Bosses pictured on Wanted Posters, he blasts the villains' flunkies . . . and also acquires various arms to help in his noble mission.

Layout: The view is from overhead as the screen scrolls top to bottom. There is also a stationary General Store screen. There are six different levels in all.

Hero: Billie Bob strolls into combat packing nothing more than the ability to walk in any direction, move from side to side, and shoot straight or diagonally. Along the way he collects stronger weapons, all of which are listed in the instructions . . . including the anachronistic Napalm Bomb (called Smart Bomb on the screen). Some of these goodies are located inside Barrels; Money (and Bullets, in later levels) are obtained by shooting bad guys; or, as Billie Bob amasses points, he can make purchases at the General Store. (He does this by talking to everyday townfolk. Each person offers a different selection of goods.) He can also find Yashichis for extra lives, and there are POWs inside some Barrels which, when grabbed, obliterate everything on the screen (these are not discussed in the instructions). Something else not mentioned in the booklet: Bob has the power to stop TNT from exploding. All he has to do is grab it as soon as it's tossed and it'll disappear.

Enemies: Twelve different kinds of foes and obstacles, as well as the Bosses, are listed in the instructions. Not mentioned are Boulders, which roll down at you from Death Mountain and can be shot for points. Most weapons fired by enemies can only reach halfway across the screen. Keep this in mind when you're trying to stay out of range of their fire!

Menu: There is only the one-player hunt.

Scoring: Bob earns from 100 to 300 points for each non-Boss enemy slain. The Bosses' bounty is listed at the beginning of each screen.

Beginner's Strategy: One of the nice things about *Gun.smoke* is that there's a different strategy to each level. Here it is over the first five levels (we'll leave the sixth for you to discover).

Hicksville: Play fairly low on the screen, so you have time to dart to the sides and get the Barrels on the building stoops. A POW can be found in a Barrel right after the first Barricade, and a Horse appears at the far end of a blue building on the right, after the first set of

Barricades. The Wanted Poster will be found shortly thereafter, by a blue building to the left, and there's a Yashichi two left-side buildings later. A second POW can be found three buildings after that, also on the left. Bandit Bill arrives now. Just stand at the bottom of the screen and shoot whenever he stands up. Dodge his bullets while he's lying down, firing at you.

The Boulders: Watch out for the bandits jumping at you from the sides; worse, you can't shoot them while they're on the hills. There'll be a Horse at the midway point, on the left. Play this round halfway up the screen, but scoot back when the guys from the side slip behind you. Toward the end play a little lower, so that you'll have time to shoot the many baddies who will be coming at you from the top of the screen. Watch for Skulls, one on the right and then on the left; the Wanted Poster is near the one on the left. When you face Cutter Boomerang, you'll really have your hands full . . . ducking at his twin Boomerangs, attempting to shoot him, and also fighting off all of Cutter's gang members. It may be some consolation that thrown Boomerangs disappear two seconds after they're tossed. All you can do here is stay on the move and keep shooting (at gang members first, since they move faster than Cutter).

Comanche Village: Watch for baddies hiding in teepees! The field really becomes crowded with enemies now, and if you haven't already, buy a Magnum or Shotgun.

Coming up quickly on the right are two Barrels; one has a Yashichi, the other a Skull. On this level you can't dart for the contents of Barrels as easily as you did before. Get below them and shoot up . . . blasting enemies as you approach the contents slowly and steadily. You'll find the Wanted Poster on the grass, roughly halfway through the level; it's lying to the left of a Skull which is itself on the left. Note: You can shoot and destroy the Axes thrown at you by Indians. When Devil Hawk appears at the end, he descends along the right side of the roadway. Go up there at once and begin shooting; when he spreads his arms, an arc of deadly blue projectiles will shower down at you. Get between them while firing at Hawk's tribe members first, then at Hawk himself when you can spare the bullets. Again, his helpers (whose ranks seem to be bottomless!) move faster than he does and must be dealt with first.

Advanced Strategy: As rough as the game became on the last level, things get rougher on level four.

Death Mountain: More cluttered with baddies than any level to date! Worse, nearly half of them come at you from behind, from the bottom of the screen. Making things even more interesting is the fact that there are Mountains on the side of the screen (left to start, then on the right); Boulders come rolling down these and must be avoided or shot. The best way to deal with this level is this: When the Mountains are on the left, play the game in the upper right, and vice versa. This will allow you to blast the baddies who come down from the top, while giving you ample room to drop back and plug the thugs who come from behind. Pretty early on, watch for three Barrels on the right; there's a POW between two Skulls. Toward the end, enemies will be so aggressive and plentiful that you have to risk getting clobbered by boulders; proceed with your back against the Mountain, just to cover your rear. You'll find the Wanted Poster very close to the end, in a row of stones. Surprisingly, the Ninja Boss is actually pretty easy to slay. He comes and goes in a puff of smoke; as soon as you see the smoke begin to materialize, shoot at it. You'll hurt him before he can hurt you.

Cheyenne River: There are Bridges and Water here, and while you can go in the Water, the current makes your Bob difficult to control. Take a dip only in case of an emergency. And before you cross a Bridge, stand on the shore and shoot out at the Water: you don't want to have too many foes popping up to the surface while you're stuck on a narrow Bridge with no room to duck and dodge! At the end, when you finally face the bomb-chucking Fatman Joe Bomb Gun (now *there's* a monicker!), you'd better have at least a Magnum in your hand!

Par: Scores vary from level to level, since the numbers of villains increases. As a rule, you'll have 30,000 points at the end of Hicksville,

85,000 after the Boulders, 150,000 following Comanche Village, and so on.

Training Tips: Your greatest asset is to know the lay of the land, and to get a good look at the terrain, you should walk through the town fully armed. How? On the title screen press the A button 4 times, hit Select 4 times, move the controller or joystick twice to the right (holding it to the right the second time), then hit Start while still holding the controller/joystick. (You have to input all of this while the title screen is still on . . . but slowly enough so that each tap registers.) When Bob appears in the street, take a look at the General Store screen . . . and savor what you've got at your disposal!

Rating: This game is similar to *Commando, Ikari Warriors,* and all of them thar cartridges . . . but the western theme is a refreshing change from all the military, mercenary clones! (Though what napalm is doing here is anybody's guess. . . .)

Challenge: B+

Graphics: B

Sound: B−

CHAPTER ELEVEN

GYRUSS

Type: Space shoot-'em-up.

Objective: By 2500 humankind has established bases on all the worlds of the solar system. Then, evil Gyrussians invade from another star system, led by the evil Genghis Khan— the selfsame tyrant from earth's past! (Why didn't the Mongol just stay here in the twelfth century? Who knows?) As you move from the outer worlds toward the sun, you and your spaceship are all that stands between freedom and enslavement for our solar system.

Layout: Your ship moves around the fringes of the screen, either clockwise or counterclockwise. All enemies come at you from the center. You must liberate all nine planets, each of which consists of three Stages of battle, as well as fight your way through various Challenge Stages.

Hero: Your ship comes with a Neo-Tutonic Cannon as well as an Ultra-Lazonic Phaser bank. As the battle progresses, you can destroy Bonus Spheres to transform your Neo-Tutonic Cannon into multifire Neo-Bomb-Blastic Cannons. Each Bonus Sphere also adds to the number of times you can fire your all-destroying Phaser (seven is the limit).

Enemies: The individual enemy "Deathships" have no names. There are also Meteors (which can't be destroyed), Amoebae (which take several hits to destroy—some of them splitting in two just to make your life miserable), small, indestructible Blossoms, and many others. The toughest foes are the Mouths: creatures with four or more maws, who can only be destroyed when these maws are open (and firing projectiles at you!). Note: When Deathships swarm onto the screen, try to get them all. If you don't, the ones you miss will cluster in the middle and come back out at you. Only this time, if they collide with your ship, you're space dust!

Menu: There is only the one-player game.

Scoring: You earn points for blasting your foes, usually just 100 points for each ship. You earn 1000 points if you destroy every ship in the first wave of a Stage, 2000 for the second wave, 4000 for the third, and so on. There are also 1000 points awarded whenever you hit bonus ships that pop up on the screen.

Beginner's Strategy: It'll be easier to get through the game if you think of the *Gyruss* screen as the face of a clock; use the numbers as landmarks, so you'll know where to go. The game begins at Neptune (which is farther from the sun, now, than Pluto). In Stage One you can defeat each successive wave by positioning yourself at 6:00, 9:00, 6:00 (watching for a Power-Up here), and 12:00 (another Power-Up will arrive). In Stage Two you have to deal with a four-mawed Mouth. The maws are located in the corners, like a square, which revolves slowly clockwise. Deal with this foe by orbiting it slowly, sticking with each maw until it's destroyed. In Stage Three go to the 6:00 position to tackle wave one, then to 9:00 for wave two . . . but be ready, in both cases, to jiggle your ship from side to side a bit, since Meteors will come swarming at you from amidst the ships. The next few waves are easy, followed by a four-mawed Mouth with openings at the quarter-hour positions. This Mouth and those that follow will be shooting at you. While you can orbit the creature and put in shots as you pass each maw, and ending up *between* mouths when the projectiles fly out, most players find it preferable to stay with one mouth until it's destroyed. Start with the one at the bottom. Shoot it, dodge to the left or right to avoid its fire, get back under it, and shoot again. Two barrages should do it. When it's destroyed, this area becomes your "safe" zone, since there are no more projectiles being spit from the exploded Mouth. Move to the next Mouth on either side, shoot it, dodge back into the safe zone when that Mouth spits, return when the projectiles have dissipated, and blow it up. Do this for all four Mouths. If you're not sure of your abilities here, use a Phaser to sizzle one Mouth to oblivion, thus creating a safe zone with no hassle. Stage Four (and Stages that are multiples of four, that is, eight, twelve, sixteen) are Chance Stages. There's no danger here, just lots of Deathships and bonuses to shoot, and Power-Ups to acquire.

When you reach Pluto (Stage Five), orbit the screen in the direction opposite the ships in each wave. It's futile to chase them; you won't catch 'em. Best to circle against them, picking them off as your paths cross. Stage Six: You'll face waves and a four-maw Mouth . . . nothing particularly troublesome until the Amoebae start coming at you. Your first few shots will accomplish nothing, but knock the creatures back. The second or third barrage (depending upon how powered-up your ship is) will destroy them. For this Stage stay mostly at the 12:00 position. Stage Seven: The Amoebae split when hit in this round, giving you twice the trouble. However, the real killer is the Planetoid. Toward the end of the round get to the bottom of the screen (the Planetoid materializes on top—if you're there, you're dead). It is going to move around the screen, spreading a string of deadly Planetesimals. You have to shoot this undulating cord; your shots turn the individual beads from green to red, rendering them harmless. However, if any of them, or the Planetoid itself, touches you, you lose your ship. Stay mostly between the 2:00 and 6:00 positions, keeping the string of Planetesimals between you and the Planetoid. Stage Eight is a Chance, with the Deathships coming in and out of the center of the screen as if they were giant yo-yos. Stay mostly at 6:00 for the best results.

Stage Nine: Go to 9:00 for the first wave, 6:00 for the second, then just race around for the rest. Instead of coming from the outside of the screen, the ships will spiral up at you from the center. Stage Ten: Another four-maw Mouth is in the center, rotating. Only this one shoots Space-Fuzzies, which move fast and in unpredictable directions. These can and must be shot. If you pay attention to the Death-ships, the Fuzzies will nail you. Stage Eleven: Shuttle between the 6:00 and 9:00 positions to start. Strings of Planetesimals and Fuzzies will come at you (the latter zigzagging all over). When Deathships start spinning out from the center, just go to the outsides, spin-ning around the screen. When the four-maw Mouth arrives, you'll find it tougher and faster-spitting than its predecessors. If you haven't already, this would be a good time to break in your Phaser.

Advanced Strategy: Stage Twelve: a Chance, little different from the Chance before. Stage Thir-teen: You get to fight the Jellyfish monsters here. They can only be slain when they turn their bottoms to you, so stay out of their way the rest of the time! Stage Fourteen: There's a four-maw Mouth here. Shoot at it between waves of Deathships; when the waves attack, just circle the screen, shooting. Stage Fifteen: Play this one mostly on the bottom. There's a six-maw Mouth at the end; use Phasers, or if your reservoir's dry, rotate the monster, shooting at the mouths. Stage Sixteen: This Chance is best handled from between the 6:00 and 9:00 positions. In Stage Seventeen, stay mostly on the bottom. Stage Eighteen: The four-maw Mouth with waves of Deathships spilling out won't be any tougher than the one you fought in Stage Fourteen. However, what will be a pain here are the Space Seeds; when you see these, dodge them but don't shoot them. Shot, they split into four separate Seeds! Stage Nineteen: This is where the game really gets serious. You have to fight an Armored Brain which circles around in the center, spitting Seeds. You've got to shoot off the Armor piece by piece without hitting the Seeds . . . but that isn't the tough part. (Just circle and shoot carefully!) When the red little Brain itself is exposed, a pair of arms come out, which whip around the screen. If they touch you, it's bye-bye. Since the arms can't reach you in the corners, tuck yourself in the corner from which the monster is farthest, shoot at it, shift to another corner when the Brain moves closer, and so on. Get in enough hits and it will die. Stage Twenty is a Chance, just a tad faster than the last one. Stage Twenty-One: Tuck yourself into the lower-right corner to shoot the Space-Fuzzies. When you have to come out of the corner, stay on the bottom or top so you'll have as much time as possible to see what's coming out at you. Generators will shortly come sailing out from the center; these are balls with an electrical arc between them. If any part of the balls or arc touches you, sayonara. You have to shoot the balls to destroy the beam, so watch as it whirls from the center, and shoot carefully! Stage Twenty-Two: Stay on the bottom to deal with the Fuzzies, most of which come from the top. The four-maw Mouth here is nothing special. Stage Twenty-Three: Start in the upper right to combat the first wave of Fuzzies, then move to the bottom. There's an eight-maw Mouth at the end, and this one is best handled by the orbiting technique; don't stop to deal with each maw, just circle the rotten alien, firing at it!

The Stages in the rest of the game can't be described; they're just too maddeningly busy! But if you've gotten this far, you're a skilled enough space pilot to continue on your own!

Par: If you're not getting as far as Jupiter, you belong in some other solar system. You should earn roughly 70,000 points for every world and its Chance Stage.

Training Tips: Because the circular gameplay is so unusual, it's a good idea to go through a few Stages just whipping around the outsides of the screen; not stopping, but spinning around, firing toward the center, simply getting used to the movement of the ship—and your enemies. It's also a good idea to draw some clock-like maps, marking where waves originate in each Stage. If you pause the game and take a glance at these, you'll know what to expect!

Rating: Playing this game is like taking a ride down a drain. But that's *good;* unless you're a

Scrubbing Bubble, it's like nothing you've ever experienced!

Challenge: A

Graphics: B+

Sound: A (there's some excellent Bach to shoot by!)

CHAPTER TWELVE

ICE HOCKEY

Type: Team sports competition.

Objective: With four players on each team, you battle for control of the Puck, from Face-off to Goal. There are three periods in each contest, with Goalkeeperless overtime if necessary.

Layout: The screen scrolls from side to side as the players skate across the ice.

Hero: Each player can assemble her or his formation from three Skaters (Thin, Ordinary, and Stocky) plus a Goalkeeper. Thin is fast on the skates but weak on shooting and body-checking; Stocky is the reverse; and Ordinary is well-balanced with both skills. Each Skater has the ability to move the puck, pass, fake a shot, and body-check. They can also be benched as a penalty (allowing the other team to mount a power play) and can learn to "flip" the puck right through the stick of another player (see instructions).

Enemies: Obviously, in a two-player game, your opponent will select her or his own team from the same three-player bench. When you play the computer, you can pick its team.

Menu: Two players can compete against each other, or one player can battle the computer. Players race against the clock and can select periods that last seven, ten, or fifteen minutes. They can also select the speed of play, from slow to insane!

Scoring: Players earn points for goals. There are also penalties for "icing" (explained in the instruction booklet) and for fighting (which automatically occurs, as explained in the booklet).

Beginner's Strategy: Everyone has their preferences, but by and large, the *best* team you can send to the ice is one consisting of three Stocky players and one Thin. This gives you strength and a dash of speed. Look at it this way: Stocky is going to overpower whoever he tangles with, and that means more shots at the Goal for you. Percentagewise, you're bound to score more this way.

In general, if you're playing the computer on the lower speeds, do a lot of passing close to the Goal, from opposite sides. The computer locks in on whoever has the Puck; a fast pass is going to leave the computer open. In faster speeds, the most successful passing you can do is bank shots, off the Sideboards. The computer player will head for the Puck, which it doesn't expect will come caroming off the side!

When playing the computer or another player, try to move in a zigzag pattern to throw your opponents off. And don't be afraid to use the area behind either Goal for a breather . . . or to fool your opponent. If you race in one way, pivot suddenly, and come back out the same way, you're sure to throw them off! Also, use your own players as a stationary block, by going around them. Lastly, if an opposing player is close to your Goal, don't be afraid to bring your Goalkeeper out to fight for the Puck. It's a gutsy move, since your opponent can shoot around you if they're sharp . . . but more than once in a while you'll catch them unaware! Speaking of the Goalie, when he makes a stop and gets rid of the Puck, have him shoot straight ahead and try to get one of your players to come up behind it. You can use the momentum of the Puck to help speed it across the ice!

Advanced Strategy: One tack to try when you're really good is, at the Goal, to feint a shot to the right or left (where the Goalie will be waiting). Then shoot quickly in the opposite direction, ricocheting the Puck off the Goalpost and into the Cage.

Another neat move is the following: If you're in a corner of the Rink, trapped, or simply looking to make a cool pass, slide the Puck along the Backboard. It will bounce off the Sideboard and end up in the Face-off Circle on the opposite side.

Par: If you've scored three Goals against the computer on the medium level (3) in a medium-length game, you're pretty good.

Training Tips: Clearly, playing against the computer at top speed (5) is going to sharpen your skills, while at the same time humbling you. Especially if you give it the same team that you've got. But for a real workout do the following: At the title screen, push the Start button, and at the *same time* press buttons A and B on both controllers. The result? You'll play without Goalies! (If you program this command while the team-selection screen is on, you will create a "Super Puck" that darts around the screen at awesome speed!)

Rating: Like *Double Dribble,* this is a terrific cartridge for the family, not only because of the competition, but because of the different levels of play. It's also a pretty faithful recreation of the hockey experience . . . right down to the Puck often being impossible to see! One drawback: Unlike *Double Dribble, Ice Hockey* doesn't have those spectacular close-up graphics of an attempted score. It would've been something to see approaching players from the Goalie's point of view!

Challenge: A

Graphics: B+

Sound: B

CHAPTER THIRTEEN

INDIANA JONES AND THE TEMPLE OF DOOM

Type: Adventure quest.

Objective: In India, adventurer-archeologist Indiana Jones learns that the evil High Priest Mola Ram has abducted the children of Mayapore. His purpose? To have them mine for jewels . . . and for the powerful, enchanted Sankara Stones. Indy's mission is to enter the Temple of Doom in order to free as many children as possible, claim the stones, and destroy Mola Ram.

Layout: The screen scrolls both vertically and horizontally. The Temple of Doom consists of twelve Waves in all, each consisting of a main chamber and a mining level. There are also Secret Doors, some of which are discussed below.

Hero: Indy begins the game with five lives, modest jumping ability, and a Whip. He can use the lash to beat enemies or swing over precipices. Along the way, Indy can acquire the various weapons described in the instruction booklet. Two of these are most important: Hats (for extra lives), and Map Pieces. A note about leaping the Lava Pools: If your Bomb has solidified only two thirds of a Pool, you can jump over the rest. Also: When you lose a life, your next Indy resumes the adventure where the last one perished. If you happen to die in a Lava Pool, your demise will usually cause part of it to solidify.

Enemies: These are discussed in the instructions. A few pointers: If time runs out, not only does Mola Ram appear and strip you of weapons and a life, you get booted to some other level. Also: When you face Attacker Thuggees (especially in Wave Nine), do your best to whip them off a ledge. They can't get back at you unless there's a Ladder nearby. If you back 'em into Lava, they won't be returning. A final note: If, when you use your Whip to swing, the arc of your swing touches a baddie, you'll frequently kill them.

Menu: There is just the one-player adventure.

Scoring: You play against the clock while gathering weapons as well as points (for foes slain and children manumitted—released from bondage).

Beginner's Strategy: In Wave One there are two routes you can take to get under way. Go left, up, then swing to the right; save the kid next to the door and reveal an arrow. Chuck a Bomb up to reveal a Secret Door. Go through to room S2. Go right. At the door, jump down. Save kids, swing to the left, save more kids, and go back to the right. Jump down, rescue more slaves, go to the lower right-hand corner; jump down to the Conveyor Belt on the left, then off to the left (do this from the very edge of the Conveyor, leaping down at roughly the 7:00 position). Take the gun, shoot the Skull, use the Whip to swing right on the Skull, and exit via the door. This will bring you to Wave Nine! Obviously, you can't just go here without having collected sundry artifacts along the way, but it's a good shortcut to Wave Nine, with which you'll need to become familiar in order to win the game.

An alternative route is to enter S2, go down, right, to the door on the right; don't go in, but swing to the left and go in the door there to reach Wave Five. Yet another path you can take: Take a door into the Mines from Wave One, immediately hop off the cart and move up. Save kids to reveal two passages; the first will show you a Secret Door to Wave Five; a slave-child to the right will give you a Blue Key which will open a Blue Door, top right. This will take you to Wave Two. If you stay in the cart and continue to the right, you'll end up back in the cave section of Wave One.

In Wave Two go right and down, saving kids. Take a door to the Cart phase; look for the Green Door to get to Wave Three. In Three you'll find a Pink Door on the Cart level (to the right) which brings you to Wave Four. When you get to Four, go down and right; a rescued kid will reveal a Secret Door which will give you access to S5. Once there, swing all the way to the right, head up, then go left.

Save the children, then go all the way to the top, sweeping left and right as you travel. A door on the top left will lead you to Wave Six. Here, make your way up and left to the doorway. In the Cart phase, a Map Piece can be found beneath the first kid to the right. Another way to handle Wave Six: Enter the door to the left of the graven animal face, which will take you to S7; climb up—the first door up, on the left, will lead you to Wave Eight.

Advanced Strategy: Wave Nine is a toughie. Go left, at once, to get a Hat from a rescued kid. Head right and up, then right and left collecting weapons. Now: There are several places to cross the Lava River. However, the best one is just above where the Conveyor Belts form an L. The Belts will protect you from the Thuggees. The only problem here is that Lava Monsters pop up with less frequency than anywhere else. Still, be patient and they *will* arrive. (Be advised: Even if you lose a life, the bridge you've constructed from dead Lava Monsters will remain. Also be advised that it's a lousy idea to try and cross dead Monsters diagonally. Just hold onto your fedora, and Monsters *will* appear for you to make a straight-ahead crossing!) It's a good idea, by the way, to kill Monsters when they appear, even if you don't need 'em. That way, when you reach that point in the crossing, you'll have a stepping-stone. You end up having to kill a few extra Monsters this way, but at least you don't have to wait needlessly.

When you get to Kali, snatch the Stones and

head to the right. The door to the Map Room is just a stone's throw away! And you'll *need* the Map, especially when you have to deal with the ubiquitous Chutes and Lava in Wave Ten! So take careful notes here, then enjoy the rest of the game; the toughest part really is over!

Par: The juncture that separates the Indys from the Imposters is the big Lava River of Wave Nine. An average player will get this far; a very good one will get beyond.

Training Tips: You only really need to become proficient in snapping the Whip, swinging, and hopping from Conveyor Belts to Carts, and vice versa. You can learn all of this in Wave One. Once you do, the only real chore you have is making a map to learn the ins and outs of the Temple of Doom. (Note: Use the shortcut to Wave Nine detailed in Beginner's Strategy. Take time to study the Lava River crossing before you have to do it "for real," in a game situation.)

Rating: The quest aspect of the game is fun, though there really isn't a lot of diversity in the villains or Indy's weapons. Once you master the few basic skills, the combative elements of the game become comparatively dull.

Challenge: C+

Graphics: B−

Sound: B+ (good musical accompaniment and some nifty sound effects)

CHAPTER FOURTEEN

IRON TANK: THE INVASION OF NORMANDY

Type: Search-and-destroy.

Objective: Before the assault on the Normandy Coast on D-Day in 1945, "Paul" of Command Unit 88, a group aka "Iron Snake," must use his mighty Iron Tank to clear the area of enemies (gee . . . that won't give Allied plans away, will it?).

Layout: The screen scrolls in all directions as you move around. There's also a map screen to tell you where you are, or should be!

Hero: Iron Tank can move in all directions; the Turret can, too, regardless of which way the Tank is facing. Your basic Tank fires Shells. However, as it drives along, you will find Power-Up items either lying on the ground or else revealed when you blow an enemy to nuts and bolts. These powers are described in the instruction booklet. Your Tank's most significant weakness: running out of Energy. Energy is one of the Power-Up objects you can find. Also hidden throughout the game are Prisoners. Save them (by picking them up or freeing them from Jails), and you will either get their thanks . . . or important information.

Enemies: In addition to the twenty-one foes listed in the booklet, you must also beware Boats shooting at you, ultra-deadly Mines (one hit, and it's bye-bye), Narrow Bridges, electricity at the Power Station (one zap, and you're toast), and other headaches.

Menu: There is only the one-player game.

Scoring: You earn or lose the above-mentioned powers and Energy as you go.

Beginner's Strategy: The most important tactic to win at *Iron Tank* is to use the scenery as protection; hide behind mountains, buildings, and so on. Dart out to fire, get back to avoid being hit, and so forth. It will spare you hits against your Tank.

Here are some directions and hints to get you started. Keep in mind, however, that after a while the only strategy is *experience.* If you can't take cover and shoot, knowing the layout of Normandy isn't going to do you any good.

To begin with, run over Soldiers. Don't feel bad: They'll destroy you if they can. When you're low on Energy, even their bullets can kill Paul! There's a Prisoner on the right of the stone maze; save him, though you won't get an intelligence from him. The Tanks here are all easily dispatched. Stay on the road to avoid the Planes when they pass overhead, and don't pay any attention to the Rocket—all it does is make a lot of noise. When you come to the Track, stay on it, hanging back, toward the bottom of the screen, while you shoot ahead. When the Track splits into three rails, stay on the one to the far right. Keep shooting ahead; you'll be relatively safe here from fire on the left.

There's a Think Tank ahead: it'll take 8 Bomb shots square on the Turret to destroy it (less, with additional weapons . . . for example, just 4 if you throw everything in your stockpile at it). When you reach the Prison compound, one freed Prisoner (on the left) will tell you how to get to Fritz, the firing train. Look for it as soon as the Track turns from silver to gold. Don't dare face it, though, unless you draw on some heavy firepower!

Advanced Strategy: As we warned you above, learn to use whatever's around for shielding. When you finally reach the Battleship (it'll be on the top of the screen), it will be absolutely necessary to hide behind the warehouses, or you're scrap metal.

In case you get clobbered once too often in certain areas, here are some code numbers that will take you to various sections of the map: 3443771, 7611510, 4239931, 3234773 (past that infernal train!), 2327660, 2322502, and 4953481 (for fun with the Power Station).

Par: A very good player will be able to make it halfway across the map.

Training Tips: Use the codes to go ahead to other levels. If you can survive at 1314761, for example, you should have little trouble elsewhere.

Rating: Some players may actually find this

game *too* difficult . . . when Tanks, Mines, and water are everywhere! But even the seasoned videogamer will never be bored.

Challenge: A

Graphics: A

Sound: A

CHAPTER FIFTEEN

LEGENDARY WINGS

Type: Science fiction shoot-'em-up.

Objective: The time: 20,000 years in the future. The situation: The supercomputer Dark, which was built to serve humankind, has turned on us, constructing robot warships and building an army of mutated monsters. Using mechanical wings given to them by the Greek god Ares, two young heroes take the few weapons that remain and set out to destroy Dark's armies and underground base.

Layout: The screen scrolls vertically through all Areas, except during Palace, Danger, and Lucky stages, when it scrolls horizontally.

Hero: In the beginning your Legendary Soldier can fly in all directions and fire meager weapons: Guns, which fire bullets straight ahead, and Missiles, which blast installations on the ground. You acquire Power-Up armaments as the game progresses. These are discussed in the instructions and also below. There are also certain parts of the terrain that, when blasted, open tunnels to Lucky zones, where you are free to acquire points and Power-Ups. These are discussed below.

Enemies: The instruction booklet lists thirty-two foes. It *doesn't* tell you that most of these are first projectiles, which are discussed below. It also doesn't discuss the Statues, Dragons, and Eye-Bosses. The Statues are figures erected in Z patterns before a Palace, and they shoot at you. In order to disable these, you must shoot each Statue head three times. A Dragon descends from the top of the screen at the entrance to every Palace. Each one spits 3 fireballs at a time in Areas One through Two, and 6 at a time thereafter. Once you get through the Palace, you face a giant rectangular beast with Eyes hanging from its flesh and a central hole that spits deadly spray. It will fire the Eyes at you; these can be shot and destroyed. However, the spray cannot be destroyed, only dodged. Worse: The monster can only be destroyed by shots to the central hole, and the hole only opens when the Eye-Boss spits at you. Another foe, though inanimate, are the walls you encounter in the Lucky, Danger, and Palace zones. If you are trapped behind a wall and it scrolls off the screen (to the left), you will be crushed and lose a life. Finally, there are giant Heads that blow winds at you: Get caught in one of these drafts, and you'll be dragged into the mouth and have to fight your way through a Danger level. There is only one Head per Area.

Menu: There are one- and two-player modes, with two heroes battling side by side.

Scoring: You earn points for blasting foes and collecting bonus items (see instructions and also below).

Beginner's Strategy: Herewith is a complete guide to making your way through all five levels. Area One: There will be a wave attacking on the right, then left, then right. Defeating these, stay on the left for a Power-Up. Go around the giant Head, which will try to draw you into a Danger Zone. The best way to get around the Heads (whose winds become increasingly more ferocious as you move from Area to Area) is to move to one side or the other and *stay* there. Rise above a gust, slow to avoid one which will be blown ahead of you, fly forward, slow if there's another blast of wind, and finally—when you've cleared the Head—dash back to the center of the screen. You'll fight a slew of Stones next: Just shoot these busts as they come flying off their stone bodies. Your next foes will be the Boomerang Cicadas: After these attack, shoot the first Cannon Tortoise on the ground. This will open a secret passageway to a Lucky. Here you have only two concerns: Make sure you blast as many walls as possible to see what goodies are inside, and make sure the walls don't scroll off the screen with you to the left, which will mash you to a pulp. When you finish the Lucky zone, you will return to the surface just about where you were before.

You'll be facing Four Wings now; they'll

shoot at you, but are easy enough to destroy. Just make sure you don't get caught behind the sculptures on the ground as they scroll off on the bottom, or you'll be crushed. Shoot the Heads off the Statues and then go to the center top of the screen, to the Palace gate, and start shooting; the Dragon will descend, and you might as well get a few early hits in. For the most part the Dragon hovers near the top of the screen, spitting its fireballs. Every now and then, however, it will dart down *fast* and try to kill you. (It does this more often and faster as the game progresses.) The best way to deal with any Dragon is to shoot it, run to one side, wait for its fireballs to dissipate, run back underneath the monster, blast it again, go to the side opposite the Dragon, wait for the fireballs to come and go, and repeat. The Dragons in Areas One through Three won't present much of a challenge.

Inside the Palace you'll fight Hide Eyes, which can't be hurt when their lids are shut. These are relatively easy to beat. When you reach the three thick brick walls (they cover all three levels of the area through which you'll be passing), shoot through the one on the bottom. Then go up, to the middle level, and duck to the left to nab the Power-Up there. At the end of the Palace you'll face the Eye-Boss. Stay on the left, in the center. The monster is going to move in that direction. (Note: At the end of each Palace, the creature will come farther and farther to the left.) When it fires its red spray, hold your ground and shoot straight ahead, through the spray; this is the only time the central eye is open and vulnerable. Drop to the bottom to get out of the way of the red death, then come up again and wait for the eye to open. Eyes will also be flying at you from the side of the monster; shoot these or duck 'em, the choice is yours. Two good, solid hits in the core will destroy the monster.

Not too tough, right? Even if you were unlucky enough to get snagged by the Head wind earlier and drawn into Danger, Area One is easy. If you end up in Danger early in the game, the Area isn't too difficult. The real problem in these zones comes when you pass over Water and a swarm of monsters hops up at you at once. When you reach these ponds, rush to the right of the screen and *stay* there to avoid the horde—shooting ahead all the while, in case something comes at you from that direction.

Area Two begins with Devil Squids raining down on you, left and right. Go to either side, destroy the monsters there, then move to the center and kill the Squids that have shifted over. Go to the bottom and shoot the Fright Eyes and Claws that follow; watch for a Power-Up after the first batch of Claws. Go around the Head as before, and after a wave of Cracks (they are much bigger than shown in the booklet!), you'll find a second Power-Up. Below, a dark blue region will be coming up soon; when it passes, watch for the Cannon on the ground, then the horizontal row of two

above it; the one on the left will let you in to a
Lucky. Descend and look for a Power-Up in
one of the first walls. When you get out,
there'll be more monsters dropping from
above, followed by more Statues, a Dragon,
and the Palace. The Palace is different here
only in that there are areas where the ceilings
are very low, and there's Lava beneath you.
Fly carefully: If you touch the Lava, you're
dead. Toward the end of the Palace you'll
have to deal with both Death Beams and
Super Suzies. The Death Beams fire down at
you; dart past them as soon as they fire a
burst. As for the Suzies, they shoot horizontally and occasionally spring up and down.
They don't fire when they spring, so that's the
best time to plug them. The Eye-Boss throws
more Eyeballs and does so faster than before.

Area Three: Lady Bugs greet you here, and
they're easy enough to shoot or dodge. Keep
an eye out for a Power-Up, which is found
around the four Cannons. By the way: Now, as
always, you should nail the Cannons as soon
as you see them. Once they're to your side, you
can't use your Missiles; all you can do is dodge
their fire. By then, Cannons may be so plentiful that you won't be able to slide between the
artillery shells! At this point your flying foes
get more troublesome than ever. Thorn Shots
arrive; most likely, you won't be able to destroy any of these before they fire their quills
at you. Thus, get in your shots, be prepared to
weave between the quills, then get close to the
Thorn Shot and shoot it again. After the Head

you'll have to deal with the very tough Horse Shoe Crabs. Each of these has a thick spine in the center, which it fires at you; a flurry of these can be tough to avoid! Fortunately, you can destroy the Spines (and, of course, the Crabs) with well-placed shots. The best way to deal with this foe is to stay on the bottom, shooting up at the creatures. If they become too plentiful, get over to the side and crawl up the wall, where the traffic won't be as thick. Firing constantly, make your way slowly back to the bottom. Next up: a series of Pyramid-like ground installations. Stay on the right; to the right of the last structure, on the ground, is a small Cannon. Destroy it and open a tunnel to a Lucky. You'll definitely *need* to go in here now, since the Power-Ups will prove crucial. When you emerge from the Lucky zone, the barrage from the Statues will be fast and constant. You'll have to keep shifting from side to side to avoid being fricasseed. At this point the Dragon starts shooting 6 fireballs at you, so getting into the Palace will be tougher than before as well. When you do get inside, just race up, down, up, down, shooting all the while to get the Hide Eyes out of the way. After killing them, stay just slightly to the left of the center of the screen, shooting whatever comes at you. Watch out for the titanic Sea Horse; once its pieces assemble, it fires a lethal beam from its tail. If you can't blast the pieces as they come together, get to the right of the monster: it can only fire to the left.

Advanced Strategy: Area Four: You're going to

have to move and weave almost constantly now, your flying skills becoming as important as your marksmanship. To begin with, you'll face heavy ground fire from all sides. Stay low and to the sides until you've taken out the Cannons. The Reflectors come next, dropping inexorably on top of you; what's difficult about these creeps is that you can't move too far to the side, since there are stationary spikes poking out from the walls. Touch 'em and perish! Just hold your ground beneath the Reflectors and keep firing at them. Another pain-in-the-wings here are the overpasses; when you go under them, you can't always see what's happening. Thus, watch what comes at you from the top of the screen and gauge how its moving, since you'll be shooting blind for brief periods. When you reach the Statues, if you don't want to risk fighting them all, stay to the far right or left. Just slide out to shoot the Statues on your side, which will eliminate enough flak to allow you to reach the Palace. Inside, the walls are close together; you've got to weave up and down quickly, or you'll be trapped as the screen scrolls left. Again, when you face the Death Beams here, stay to the left and dash to the right only after they have discharged a deadly ray. Upon encountering the horde of Fly Bees, stay to the left and shoot right.

Area Five: You'll get a Power-Up right away, and another follows quickly. For the first part of this level stay on the very bottom of the screen. After passing the Head, stay on the right, ducking into the center to fire at the multitude of enemies, then getting back to the side when the air is just too thick with them. When the Horse Shoe Crabs arrive, go to the bottom again and deal with them as before. When you reach the first group of horizontal walls, look for the Cannon on the ground after the last wall; the Cannon on the left conceals a Lucky tunnel. When you leave the Lucky zone, you'll have to knit around more walls, deal with more Statues, another Dragon, and the Palace monsters. The vertical walls of the Palace are particularly harrowing; they're solid, and you must race up and down them, firing along their entire length, in order to find the weak spot and blast through. If you don't do this quickly enough, you'll be pulverized as they scroll to the left. When you reach the Eye-Boss at the end, it's going to come so far to the left you'll swear it's going to crush you. But it won't. Just stay in the middle, firing at the core, dropping down when necessary to avoid its crimson spray. However, this time, when the central eye explodes—stay in the center of the screen and keep firing! You have to shoot your way *through* the monster this time, and when you've blasted out the other end, you must battle the Giant Eye. This monster is a small one, and a bit of an anticlimax: It vanishes and materializes in different areas, shooting at you all the while. But the projectiles are a cinch to avoid, and the Eye is easily killed with a few shots. Upon winning (and sitting through a tedious listing of the game programmers), you will find yourself back at the beginning of the game—though with all the powers you had at the end of Area Five.

Par: A good player should be able to score 200,000 points in every Area, making for a total of one million points by game's end.

Training Tips: Especially in Areas Four and Five, being able to duck and dodge is extremely important. Play the game without firing any weapons, just maneuvering your hero through the various obstacles. If you can do this successfully, you'll surely triumph when you play the game for real!

Rating: This game combines the magic of the Greek myth of Icarus and Daedalus with the best gameplay aspects of *Alpha Mission* and *Gradius.* A few more levels would have been nice, though.

Challenge: B

Graphics: A

Sound: B (wing-flapping sounds and whistling wind would've made this even more special)

CHAPTER SIXTEEN

MAGMAX

Type: Futuristic shoot-'em-up.

Objective: Aliens have conquered our world, and humans are being slaughtered by the evil Computer Babylon. To survive, humans create a transformable robot named MagMax. Unfortunately, MagMax's parts are spread all over the landscape. As a brave human, your task is to assemble the robot's pieces and fight the enemy.

Layout: The screen scrolls horizontally. There are six kinds of terrain: overground, underground, oversea, undersea, the base surface, and the base interior.

Hero: You begin your journey as a simple flying machine, which fires just one stream of "energy beams." As you acquire body parts, you become a robot that shoots simultaneously from each segment of its humanoid body.

Enemies: Twenty-eight different foes are all pictured in the instruction booklet; the few that are not are nothing special.

Menu: One or two players can play alternately.

Scoring: You earn points for destroying foes (these are not elaborated upon in the instructions). Some are worth 100 points (for example, Ricks, Dahls, Speeders), some 200 (Bazarmis, Ojas, Machinery, Eaglams), and some 300 (Lisers, Biggs, Satherns, Gilburns, Hoppers, Revolvers). If you clobber an enemy with a Rock Icicle, you earn 1000 points; if you skewer two, three, or more with the same icicle, you earn 1000 points each. If you kill a foe with a Black Shell released from a Multiheaded Cannonball, you earn 1000 points per hit. You are awarded 5000 points for killing a Babylon Monster. Shooting an Atomic Symbol (see Beginner's Strategy) earns you 1000 points.

Beginner's Strategy: To begin, stay near the top, blast the Rick, move to the center, shoot the other Rick, drop to the bottom, nail the Gilburn, then rise to shoot the next four Ricks. There's a Head (actually, a head and torso) beyond; get it, then descend through the next Warp Hall. This will take you underground, where you can claim your Legs and Wave Beam Gun. Don't worry if you lose these in combat—another of each follows quickly. However, if you *don't* lose them, you're in for a surprise; shoot the next Head and an Atomic Symbol will emerge. As you proceed underground, you'll face waves of Dromae and other not-very-taxing foes . . . until the Speeders come along. These *are* difficult to beat. If you just have your ship segment and don't feel like fighting, go to the very bottom; the bullet-spitting mechanical birds can't get you here. If you want to fight, you can do one of three things (this holds true for every wave of Speeders). Since Speeders approach in roughly parallel rows, toward the top and bottom, you can stay in the center, moving up and down to shoot them when there are no bullets flying at you. However, this is tough if you have your full body, as there simply isn't enough room to maneuver. Thus, ride up and over or down and under the wave (whether it's coming low or high, respectively). Shoot while you move, and your blasts will certainly clip a few of the monsters. Finally, if you want, you can simply play three quarters of the way across the screen, close to the right side. This will get rid of the monsters before they can fire. The danger in this strategy is that if any foe gets past you (not the Speeders, which can't turn around), it can double back and destroy you from behind. You, alas, can't turn to the left! The three quarter strategy is the best for Speeders; just make sure you move back to the center when the wave passes. (If you *don't* play three quarters to the right, keep an eye on the Icicles. Since the Speeders fly one atop the other, you can make a shish kebab of a bunch of them with a single Icicle.)

Whether you stay underground or go overground hereafter doesn't much matter; eventually you'll meet the Babylon Monster. For such a formidable-looking creature, it's pretty easy to zonk. all it takes is about 40 hits. Its own fire is easy to dodge, so it won't present much of a problem.

Advanced Strategy: After the first Babylon Monster you'll face a water stage. If you have a full body, the oversea trail is best, since you won't face Underwater Currents. If you're incomplete and can weave through the Currents, go underwater; above, the Lisers, which rise suddenly from the water, are a danger! (You'll have an easier time by far if you've got the Wave Beam Gun here; you can just vaporize the Lisers and everything else in your way as you march ahead.) When you reach the base region, if you go inside, you'll find three levels—stay on the middle one. You'll have time to shoot the Hoppers, most of which bounce up from the bottom, and you'll also be able to spot the Gauses, which come at you vertically from above. If you travel on the surface of the base, Eaglams will attack, but are easy enough to shoot. The next Babylon Monster you meet can be killed like the first, though it's protected by a ship that will be shooting at you while you try to slay its master. Just concentrate on the Babylon Monster, and your fire will invariably obliterate its pesky companion.

Next up: On the surface, Eaglams will now be joined by Biggs, which dash all over the screen. You'll have to face the next Babylon Monster in the dark (don't sweat it, the monster is still visible), after which there's more water . . . with a tossed salad of monsters, as

Revolvers, Ojas, and Gippos bound all over the place. We've taken you as far as we can. Your survival here and wherever you go, for the rest of the game, is going to depend *entirely* on speed and marksmanship.

Par: A modestly-skilled player will earn 45,000 points per level.

Training Tips: It would be a good idea to run through the game with just one body part. This will hone your shooting skills. It will also let you study the two waves that are toughest to do with a full body: the Speeders and the Underwater Currents. With just a ship segment you'll zip through these with ease.

Rating: Though there are other robot games on the market *(RoboWarrior* and *Robocop)*, this one is the best for the entire family, and, quite frankly, has the coolest robot.

Challenge: B

Graphics: B

Sound: B

CHAPTER SEVENTEEN

MILON'S SECRET CASTLE

Type: Fantasy quest.

Objective: When the Evil Warlord from the north region of the land of Hudson takes over Secret Castle and imprisons Queen Eliza, hearty young Milon resolves to rescue her. Not only must he find his way around the Castle, he must also fight the many monsters with which the Warlord has stocked it.

Layout: The screen scrolls horizontally and vertically, depending upon which way Milon moves within the castle rooms. There are many chambers, each of which has its own unique menace. . . .

Hero: Milon has a magic Bubble that allows him to kill monsters. He can also jump and bop overhead objects with his head. Along the way he can gain other powers, which are described in the instruction booklet. Not mentioned are the weapons and goods he can buy in the Shop, which are discussed below. Also not talked about in the instructions is the green Boxing Glove: If Milon hits it with his head, it shrinks him, enabling him to squeeze into tight spots for goodies.

Enemies: Various nameless Monsters crawl or fly around the chambers, and you'll face fireball-breathing Demon-Monsters in select rooms. When the latter die, they bequeath you a Crystal Ball, each of which enhances the strength of your Bubbles as well as the distance they can reach.

Menu: There is only the one-player game.

Scoring: Milon collects coins, with which to buy things in the Castle's hidden shops; he also gathers (and loses) Energy. Energy is provided by Hearts (which appear when monsters are slain) and Honeycombs.

Beginner's Strategy: A few comforting facts about this game: The Monsters are easy to destroy, as videogame Monsters go; and even if you are hurt by them, Energy is relatively plentiful. The real hazard in *Milon's Secret Castle* are the Trap Doors, which can really throw you for a loss if you tumble down the wrong one.

Herewith is a *complete* guide to the first few rooms and several Demon-Monsters. The run-of-the-mill Monsters are easily slain with Bubbles; we won't bother discussing those.

You start the game on the left side of the screen. Note this position: You'll be back here again. Go in the first door, head right to the 3 Blocks, blast the 2 on either side for Coins. *Remember the location of the third Block.* You won't get far in this game without it. Go up 6 ledges to the mass of Blocks on the left. Four of the Blocks there contain Coins. Keep killing Monsters while you're here; eventually a Key will turn up. Get it, go down one level, head right, then go up to the ledge on the right. Hit the 4 Blocks on the right wall for Coins. Go back to where you got the first 4 Coins, get on top of that mass and jump to the right ledge; the platform above contains 6 Coins. Now, go back to that third Block on the ground, the important one mentioned above. Push the Block to one side or the other for 5 seconds. The Block will move; shoot where it used to be, and a Door will appear. Enter . . . but only if you've collected 16 Coins. Buy the Magic Boots and get the hints (you perform all these functions by bopping buttons with your head). Leave the room, go up 5 levels to the platform under the 3 green Windows. Shoot the third Block from the left, underfoot, to release the Hudson Bee. Grab it for a period of invulnerability. Go left. See the room with the door overhead? You can't get in there now, but here's what you do. Go to the ledge *beneath* that room, head left, and jump all the way down the pit (be sure you're ready to kill the Monsters down there). Shoot the Block on the right to get a Honeycomb. Then go up to the right (where the 6 Coins were) and go in the door.

You're outside again. Go right to the last door. Enter and go up one ledge—shoot the solitary Block overhead and get the Coin. Do the same on the next two ledges above. When you reach the third ledge, shoot the top of the wall on the right. Get the Coin, but don't go through the passageway you'll have blasted. Continue up, getting all the sing-Block Coins overhead. Go right on the top ledge; there's a Coin in the top Block of the Column. There's also a pit on the right; jump down it, into the next room. There's a huge Pyramid of Blocks to the right. Don't climb it yet, just walk to the right, shooting. The bottom two rows of Blocks in the Pyramid can be destroyed. At the very end is a Key; get it. Go left and climb, now, to the top of the Pyramid. At the top face right and shoot; a door will appear. Enter and you're outside once more. Go left to the next door, which is the Shop; buy Potion and get the hints. Exit.

Go right, once again entering the last door. Climb the ledges to the top. Obtain Energy by killing Monsters if you need it, then jump down and go back to the Pyramid. Climb, but only until you are high enough to leap to the platform on the left. Go up one more ledge and jump on the Bench while shooting to the right. (Because you bought the Magic Boots, the Benches in the rooms will allow you to jump super high, on Springs.) A Bee will appear, which is helpful to have, as you must soon face the first Demon-Monster. Jump up to the next platform, which is on the right, then hop up to the one on the left. Shoot the top Block of the Column on the left for a Honeycomb, then jump to the ledge on the right and bounce up to touch the Boxing Glove. You'll shrink; face right, shoot to make an

opening, go through it, and blast all the
Blocks you can for a fortune in Coins. Go
right, shoot the two bottom Blocks, enter the
Shop, and get the hint without making any
purchases. Leave, shooting your way out
through the Blocks on the left. (Although
these are the same ones you Bubbled your
way through before, there are no Coins now.)
Push on the last Block on the left for 5 seconds
and you'll fall through the floor. Go all the
way down to the door on top of the Pyramid.
Enter. Once more you're outside. Go left to the
window. Enter and fight the Demon-Monster
on the right. You may have to jump up now
and then to avoid its fireballs, but by and large
you'll be staying on the ground, scuttling from
side to side, shooting at it while moving in a
steady rhythm to avoid the purple flames.
When the Demon-Monster dies, get the Crystal Ball and go through the door on the right.
(If you really want to boost your score, die
here after getting the Crystal. Before you continue, hit one of the fire buttons—use turbo, if
you have it—and your score will increase a
bunch!)

Inside this new room run to the right
Speedy Gonzales *fast,* because the floor beneath you collapses! (Note where you are:
You're going to have to come back here in a
moment.) Your first order of business is to
search for a Music Box right above the floor
with the moving Black Holes. When you get it,
you'll be spirited to a Bonus Room, where you
collect everything but the flats (which look

like b's). Whether you get it or not, here's how to continue your journey from the collapsing floor. Go right to the platform with the two small Columns on it. Fall through the Trapdoor to the Trapdoor on the level below, but get off that second Trapdoor fast (head to the right) before it opens. Shoot to the right; a Door will appear (there are also 2 Coins in the Column to the right of the Door). Don't go in the Door; instead, drop, now, through the Trapdoor. Go right, touch the Boxing Glove, and go up to the ledge on the right. Jump up, facing left, and shoot the hanging Column for Coins. Go right. Shoot up at the second and third Block from the left as well as the one above it. That last one has a Coin. It also opens a passage; hop into the small cubbyhole to the right of where the upper Block was. Shoot the Block at the bottom of the wall to the right. Don't go in; go right, shoot the Blocks in the floor, drop to the ledge below, head right, and shoot the right wall for Coins. Turn left, go up the ledge with three steps, and at the top shoot the floor—the third Block from the left. It's a Trapdoor. Drop and shoot the bottom of the right wall for a Honeycomb. (Note: You must be shrunken in order to get this, and in order to continue much beyond this.) The roof of this little chamber has Coins too.

Go left through the Trapdoor, climb back up to the top of the three steps, and go to the left (avoiding the Trapdoor, this time). Jump off at the left and hit the Invisible Spring. Stay on it, gaining height, until you can reach the sole Block on the upper left. Shoot the Block to the left for Coins and to reveal a Door. Enter the Shop for free Coins and a hint. Leave, fall back to where you first started in this room, go through the moving Black Holes below to where the Blocks spell HUDSON. Go to the H and D and shoot them for Coins. You'll also find a Key here, usually between the O and N. Go to the bottom of the right wall. This is a Shop; enter and get both the hint and the Vest, which helps protect you from harm. Return to the (gold) Door you uncovered before (in the room with the Trapdoors). It'll take you, yet again, outside the Castle. This time go two Doors to the left. Once in the room, fall through the Trapdoors to the bottom. Shoot the Blocks on the left and get 4 Coins. Go right, jump on the Spring at the far right, and climb to the mass of Blocks overhead. Shoot these. Climb to the top ledge and go left. Shoot the Column, then shoot left to reveal a Door. Drop down at the end of the ledge to the platform below. Go under the ledge you were just on, stand at the Window (so you're superimposed over it), and first shoot the floor left and right for Coins. Get them, then go back to the Window and jump up, hitting your head on the bottom of the ledge. This will reveal a Music Box. Get it, and get as many points as you can in the Bonus Round.

You'll be back at the start of the room now. Go back to the upper left. Drop down to the ledge at the left of the Trapdoors. There are two rows of Trapdoors here. Jump down the *farther* row, on the right. This will deposit you on the ledge; the nearer row of Trapdoors will plunk you onto the floor! On that ledge, jump up to the spot between the Columns. Leap over the two sets of Trapdoors to the Column, shoot it, go through, and jump the last set of Trapdoors. There's a Trapdoor beyond that . . . which isn't a Trapdoor at all, but a Spring! Boing yourself up to the ledge and climb to the platform on top of the mass of Blocks. Shoot left at the Column and get the Coin; shoot left at the Block and it opens a Shop Door. Enter, get hints, and buy the Light. Leave and go left. Fall down through the two rows of Trapdoors, shooting and watching out for the Hudson Bee. Face right and shoot the Column, near the top; a Honeycomb is there. Get it, then go to the top of the Column and shoot the mass of Blocks on the right for Coins. (Note: If you haven't found a Key in here by now, hidden in the Blocks, look for it back where you first arrived in this room.) Leave via the door on the upper left.

Advanced Strategy: Yet again you're outside the Castle. But things are going to change a bit; head to the right and jump in the Well. When you hit bottom, go left and touch the Boxing Glove. Head right and jump up 7 levels on the dark blue Blocks. Jump up to the two dark blue Blocks on the left, trying to land on the one at the left. (The right one contains an Invisible Spring. *Avoid it!*) Jump up, shooting out two Blocks on the left wall (the ones partly hidden by your Energy meter). Jump into the opening. Enter the Fire Room and, using the Invisible Holes in the floor, drop to the very bottom. Shoot the solitary Blocks overhead for Coins and go right into a new room. Jump down to the right, then up to the right (where the Fire is). Go over the stump there, jump to the ledge on the right, leap to the ledge beneath that, then get yourself to the ledge beneath that, and then to the one beneath *that.* Face right: At the three-layered wall, shoot your way through. Climb the ledges, go right (keeping a keen eye out for the Hudson Bee), and go through the Fire. Drop to the ledge below, go left through more Fire, shoot the Column at the end, drop down, go right for just a bit, stop and shoot the floor, second Block from the left. Drop down to the bottom, and you'll notice a Fire Monster hovering overhead. Make your way to the right, being careful to avoid the Monster's flaming breath. Shoot the Fire atop the Column and get the Honeycomb you'll uncover. Then Bubble blast the Column the Fire was on; you'll fall through a hole into the lair of the Demon-Monster. Battle this scaly crumb like you fought the first one. Get the Crystal Ball and pass through the Door on the right, into a Shop. Buy the Hammer here. This is a *must.*

When you leave the Shop, there's an Invisible Spring in the middle of the Fire on the ledge overhead. Jump up to the left, then up to the right, then up to the left again, then across to the right to the ledge with *one* Fire burning on it. Shoot the right wall for Coins. Climb up on the right to the top and head left to where you first entered the Fire Room. Leave, and you'll be in a new room. Jump up to the third Block on the right, then to the ledge above on the right, and shoot up and left to the fourth Block of the roof. There's a Honeycomb here. Jump onto the Column beneath the Honeycomb in order to get it. Ascend, go out on the right, head back to the green Boxing Glove, climb back up the dark blue Blocks on the right, and leave the room.

Where are you? Yes . . . outside the Castle again. Now, go back to where you started the game. Go right and skip onto the second ledge. Thanks to the Hammer, you can bash through the wall (manipulating the controls as if there were a Door here). You're in a Shop; purchase the Saw, leave, and enter the room where you fought the first Demon-Monster. Go through that room, to the exterior of the Castle; make your way to the far right, to the black Window. Enter, and battle the third Demon-Monster as you did the ones before. Make sure you have all your energy when you do; if not, go into a room where there were Monsters and get some. Though the Coin supply isn't ever replenished, the new Monsters you'll slaughter always have Hearts for you!

There are more rooms to explore and conquer, but we don't want to spoil your enjoyment of the game. If you've made it to the third Demon-Monster, you're well-equipped to continue on your own. But a word of caution! Until you're an ace at handling Miron, stay out of the gray Tower to the left of the Castle proper. It's a killer den of mazes and traps!

Par: Once you know the secret of moving the stone in the first room, getting through to the second Demon-Monster is par. In musical Bonus Rooms, if you get between 40 and 50 points, you're doing okay!

Training Tips: If you're not adept at jumping from Block to Block, that will be your downfall. Practice this ability in the early rooms before moving on. It wouldn't hurt to hone your Bubblemanship while you're here either.

Rating: This is a fanciful and delightful game, one that requires thought and a diligent hunt for clues. It's sort of like *Super Mario Brothers Meets Solomon's Key,* and is sure to please fans of both.

Challenge: A
Graphics: A
Sound: B

CHAPTER EIGHTEEN

M·U·S·C·L·E·

Type: Tag-team wrestling match.

Objective: You select a fighter and undertake to beat the leotards off your opponent!

Layout: The screen scrolls slightly in all directions, depending upon how you move. You progress to fights in three different kinds of Rings: normal, an Ice Ring with a slippery mat, and an Electrified Ring with shocking Ropes.

Hero: Each wrestler is described in the instruction booklet. There's also a Booster Ball which, when flung into the ring, grants the fighter a special power unique to that player (these are also described in the instructions). The Boosters come just about equally, from the top and bottom. (Note: If you're Booster-powered and tag your teammate, you will pass the Power-Up to them.) Keep in mind that you lose Energy not just from hits delivered by your opponent, but also by your own moves. So try not to go from a Flying Body Attack to a bellyflop on the canvas too often!

Enemies: Same as the heroes. If you play the computer and keep on going, the NES's fighters get tougher.

Menu: One player can fight the computer, or two players can try to pin each other to the mat.

Scoring: You earn points for the degree of pain and suffering you inflict on your adversary. Bonus points are also awarded, depending upon the size of your victory. You fight against time, the clock counting down from 30 in each round.

Beginner's Strategy: You don't need us to tell you that specific strategies depend upon who you're fighting—in terms of both the character and the skills of your human foe. But there are some general rules.

When the Trainer appears, you know the Booster will follow. Your opponent is likely to focus on getting it; use this time to beat the living daylights out of them, instead of jockeying for position. Too many players waste time dancing around each other instead of wrestling. If you do catch the Booster, use a zigzag technique; your adversary will probably be running to stay away. You're better off trying to hit them by sweeping across the Ring than chasing them down. If you *do* get them, stay right by and hit them again. A hit from a Booster-powered Wrestler will usually cost an opponent *two* of their Energy Balls on the gauge.

A basic combination that works really well

for most of the Wrestlers is to employ a Back Drop in the middle of the Ring. Stand by your adversary, and as soon as the groggy sot rises, Back Drop them again. (The reason you have to be in the middle of the Ring is that there's no room for repeated Back Drops as you near the Ropes!)

Incidentally, in the early going against the computer, if you just stand by the ropes, it'll usually (literally) fall for a Flying Body Attack.

Advanced Strategy: If you're down to one Energy Ball on your gauge, walk toward the ropes and try to lure your opponent over. Weak as you are, you can still launch a hearty Flying Body Attack and hurt them. Then, tag your teammate. Most times, if you're down to one Energy Ball and tag your companion, the fresh Wrestler will enter the ring with four Energy Balls.

A note about the Flying Body Attack: Most players tend to back away when an opponent is obviously going to try one of these. Try not to. If you can move to one side or hop to avoid it, you can race to the Ropes, launch one, and clobber your adversary when they're just getting up from their failed attempt!

Caution: Unless you're very good, don't be Geronimo on the Ice. Unless he's standing perfectly still, it's tough to throw with precision!

Par: A good match that goes the distance should end with a score not greater than 75,000 for the winner, 50,000 for the loser. Anything beyond that means the players aren't evenly matched!

Training Tips: First, watch the M.U.S.C.U.L.A.R. computer play alone. You'll see what impressive moves can be made! Then, fight the computer—but let the machine get the Booster Balls. If you can hold your own under these conditions, you'll be ready for almost any opponent.

Rating: There are some nice special effects, and the characters *do* look like their doughy Mattel toy counterparts. Maybe that's the problem. It's not always easy to move your chubby proxy with precision, or to see whether they're doing what you want them to do! This detracts from the sweatin', gruntin' fun a bit. However, the Booster moves (especially that of Muscle Man) are a riot!

Challenge: B (vs. the computer)

Graphics: B—

Sound: C (some individualized sounds or remarks from the characters would have been swell)

CHAPTER NINETEEN

1943: THE BATTLE OF MIDWAY

Type: Dogfights and air-to-sea combat.

Objective: At the controls of a P38, you must help the Allies defeat the Japanese at the Battle of Midway.

Layout: The screen scrolls from top to bottom. There are many different Waves, all of which take place over the sea with varying degrees of cloud cover and enemy configurations. Each Wave consists of two phases, the last of which ends with a confrontation between your aircraft and some extremely powerful enemy vehicle.

Hero: Your airplane comes equipped with the ability to maneuver or travel at different speeds and also to fire bullets. Not revealed in the instructions: If you hold down the B button, you fire a laserlike blast. On the debit side, you run out of Energy points: roughly one per second of flying time; 2 per bullet hit; and 9 for colliding with another aircraft. Along the way you capture various Bonus

Characters in the air and thus gain extra weapons, points, or Energy. These are revealed by shooting at them; there will be no indication that they are there, other than sparks flying when your bullets strike apparently vacant sky. Keep shooting and the Bonus Character will materialize. Not mentioned in the instructions: You can nab a Dragonfly, which will give you two extra Power Points (see Beginner's Strategy), an Elephant (pink, naturally) for extra points, and other goodies. You only get one P38 per game, though you may continue at the beginning of the last Wave.

Enemies: Airplanes and ships of varying power. Many of these are discussed below (none are described in the instructions).

Menu: There is just the one-player game.

Scoring: You earn points for shooting down enemies and collecting Bonus Characters, and bonus Energy for completing a Wave.

Beginner's Strategy: For most of the game you'll be fighting from a position roughly two thirds of the way from the top. The only exception should be the end of Wave Six (see below). At the beginning of the game you are asked to choose how to distribute three Power-Up Points. Load them all into Offensive Power. Continue doing so each time you acquire a Power-Up Point (you'll automatically return to the Power-Up screen when you do so). When that option is full, start loading Defensive Power. Obviously, as you play, try to shoot the Red Planes; this is the way you get the

POW sign. When this appears, you can collect it . . . or you can shoot it. As you shoot it, it will change to different signs. Stop firing when you get to the one you want. (These signs are explained in the instructions.) Don't, however, rush right over to nab the POW object if it's on another side of the screen. Chew your way over, firing as you go; it's pointless (literally!) to get hit by the enemy and lose Energy in a reckless dash to gain Energy! Note: Music starts to play when you are down to your last 20 or so Energy Points. Then make it your top priority to find and hit a Red Plane.

Here's a guide to the first three Waves.

Wave One: There's a Cow hidden on the second ship. Otherwise, this is a simple, very uncluttered Wave.

Wave Two: Green planes come at you left, right, then center. A big plane will soon appear on the right. This one, and other large aircraft like it, require multiple hits to destroy. At the start of phase two, planes will come down in a weaving pattern; shoot them as they cross over one another, getting you two for one. A Battleship will quickly appear on the left of the screen. Get over and start shooting up before it appears, so you can destroy its Turrets. There's a Cow in the second ship on the left. At the end of the level you'll face a large Aircraft Carrier; you have to destroy the rows of Turrets on both sides of the ship. Weave back and forth, taking out the Turrets nearest you—a maneuver that also lets you plug the planes taking off from the middle. Note: If you have a steady hand, try pressing and holding the B button and zapping every Turret on one side with your Laser blast.

Wave Three: Start on the left and shoot up; you'll nail the many squadrons that come pouring in from this side. After that attack, start weaving left to right, spraying gunfire. If the skies get too crowded, hit your A button for a blast of Lightning to get rid of the small aircraft (Lightning doesn't affect the larger planes). When you get POWs, use them for Shotgun; that's handy, and you probably won't need Energy since there's a Yashichi on the left, halfway through the Wave. At the end of the battle you're going to face what is quite honestly the toughest of all the end-of-Wave foes: the massively huge Bomber. If you don't have all your Offensive Power Power-Ups, you're in deep yogurt. You're behind the aircraft, and you've got to knock out the four engines and cockpit while tail Turrets are gunning for you. You have a few seconds before the plane's gunfire starts, and you should use this time constructively; let loose a few flashes of Lightning and shoot the engines *at once*. To avoid flak, slide from side to side, rising slightly at each side so you can get over the bullets that reach to the end of the screen. Swing back in then, toward the plane, fire again, and repeat this maneuver on the opposite side. Note: Before you encounter the plane (when the screen turns solid blue) go to the right and shoot at nothing. An Elephant will appear.

Advanced Strategy: Wave Four: Ignore the first island in the center. At the second, smaller one, there's a Cow. Nothing terribly challenging here. In the second phase a ship will come up on the left; get its Turrets. There's a Barrel hidden at the end of this vessel. Next up is a Carrier on the right; swing left to right, shooting both sides and also moving with the ship as it moves toward the left. Note: If you don't do enough damage to the vessel, you'll be kicked back to the beginning of phase two, Wave Four.

Wave Five: An Elephant appears on the right fairly quickly. Also, beware: A few planes will come from behind you in this Wave, up from the bottom of the screen. This is the Wave when you should start Powering-Up your Defense. In phase two you'll face Swarmers—planes that zigzag down the center of the screen. Again, when they overlap, blast 'em. Next up, on the right, is a ship; use the B Laser to disable the Turrets on both sides, or just swing back and forth doing the job with regular bullets. At the end of the Wave is an Aircraft Carrier; deal with it the same as you did at the climax of Wave Two.

Wave Six: Shoot ahead on the left for the very potent Dragonfly. In this Wave you're going to have to play relatively high on the screen; half the Japanese air force is going to be coming up at you from behind! When they appear, swing back, shoot them, then get back

to the center. If you miss a few, don't be surprised—there are *that* many! The end of this
Wave is actually pretty wimpy, as Bombers
creep up on your tail. Deal with them as described above.

Wave Seven: Just before the first cloud bank,
shoot at the indentation near the center of the
screen for an Alpha. Nothing else in this
phase, except for a lot of enemy ships! In
phase two there's a ship on the left. Shoot the
Turrets. The final attraction here is a *very*
tough Aircraft Carrier which sends up a lot of
planes and a lot of Flak. If you need additional help, here's how you can get a super-
weapon. Push down the B button until you
hear a whistle. Release the button and you
will have super-powerful bullets! You
shouldn't need these anywhere except at the
end of a Wave.

Par: A decent player will collect at least 100,000
points for each wave.

Training Tips: If you want to polish your skills,
hop to different levels for a workout! Here are
the codes to go straight to advanced play. To
Wave Two, 7GI17; Wave Three, EG013 (that's
"zero" and "one"), E4I13 (that's the letter I
and then one); Wave Four, LBI1A (I, one);
Wave Five, S0I1N (zero, I, one); Wave Six,
ZDI1X (I, one); Wave Seven, IRI1D (I, r, I,
one).

Rating: This has all the challenge of a space
game like *Alpha Mission* and *Zanac,* with the
unique World War II setting and graphics. It's
a bit wacky to find Cows and Barrels in the

air, but what the hey? It's fun! It's also weird—
playing a game about a monumental Japa-
nese defeat on Japanese hardware. . . .
Challenge: B+
Graphics: A
Sound: A

CHAPTER TWENTY

OPERATION WOLF

Type: Hunt-and-destroy shoot-'em-up.

Objective: Americans have been taken hostage in the tiny South American nation of Cherigo. Your mission is to save as many of them as you can and get them to the plane waiting to carry you home.

Layout: There are four levels, each of which consists of six combat zones, all of which scroll from side to side. These zones are the same in each level, though they become increasingly difficult. The zones are: the Communication Center, the Jungle, the Village, the Ammunition Dump, the Prison Camp, and the Airport. *However,* what's different about this game is that your proxy player *isn't* on the screen. You're looking out through the soldier's eyes, and you have to shoot what you see as you move ahead (using the light gun or joystick). See Advanced Strategies for a special screen!

Hero: You are the commander of Wolfpack, the team the President has dispatched to Cherigo.

One commando fights at a time, though other Wolfpack soldiers are there to replace him if he dies. You parachute in, armed only with a gun. As you move through the zones, you can pick up extra Magazines for your weapon; extra bullets (obtained by shooting Vultures or Pigs; nice place to hide them, huh?); Dynamite which wipes out everything on the screen; a clip of rapid-fire bullets which lasts for ten seconds; a Power Drink which reduces your injury level; grenades; and extra grenades (stuck inside chickens . . . which is an even dumber place than the pigs).

Enemies: Your foes are armed differently in each zone. As you proceed, you'll face Soldiers, Armored Cars, Helicopters, Gun Boats, Motorcycles, and the General, a cur who uses a hostage as a shield. There are also civilians and prisoners: if you're careless (or heartless) and hit them, your injury level increases.

Menu: There is only the one mission.

Scoring: The points you get for destroying Soldiers and vehicles are described in the instruction booklet. Also, the more prisoners you've saved, the more money you're paid—you crass mercenary! (See Par.) During the game you have limited supplies of ammunition and physical strength.

Beginner's Strategy: Your enemies appear in roughly the same order and make the same moves from game to game. The most important thing to remember is that the vehicles take several shots to destroy: five hits for the armored car, five for the Gun Boat, and ten for the Helicopter (it takes more for the HIND Helicopter, but you'll be too busy to count: just fire with heavy artillery). Among the soldiers, when a Guerilla Soldier sneaks up from either side (they're the ones who appear closest to you, and start messing with you in the Village), stop what you're doing and get them. You'll have just five seconds until they attack —and they can be deadly. As for the General, you have to pick him off from behind his captive. Enough of the coward is sticking out on one side or the other (usually on the left) to give you a shot. As for a general shooting pattern, here's what you do: sweep back and forth, slowly, firing when you have a target, rising in a small curve to go over civilians. (Make sure that when you go around them, you go *over* and not *under* civilians. Why, you ask? The Helicopters, boats, etc., are almost always above your position. Thus, you can shoot at them while at the same time avoiding innocent bystanders.)

Advanced Strategy: If you get as far as the Ammunition Dump, you're doing okay. The thing to watch out for here is that the Helicopters come in greater numbers than before, so be prepared to cripple 'em. Please note, though: If you destroy a Helicopter with a Grenade, it will cause a much greater explosion. If a civilian is nearby, he or she may be killed. Thus, use your Gun in those circumstances. After this screen, you'll get to fight in what we affectionately call the Enemy-Spots-You screen. That's when the creeps come rushing out at you from the tall grasses. All you have to do here is keep up a steady fire and sweep from side to side, just below the center of the screen.

Par: Things don't really get tough until the Ammunition Dump, where the enemy soldiers are especially hard-nosed. An average player should be able to make it midway through this level. You should have earned 70,000 points by the beginning of the Village, 80,000 by the end of the Ammunition Dump (remember, things are getting tougher!), and 125,000 by the end of the first level.

Training Tips: The ultimate success of your mission depends upon your marksmanship. This is particularly true when an enemy soldier is holding an innocent person in front of them. It's best to perfect your fire by shooting slightly wide of the enemy and inching closer on successive shots. You may die, but you'll soon learn just how wide of the enemy you can fire and still kill them—without harming the hostage. Spend time in the Communication Center, and especially in the Jungle, honing your sharpshooting abilities. Once that's become second nature—and it *better* be, if you're going to be able to shoot enemies *and* collect the weapons scattered about the field—you'll be in good shape to complete the mission.

Rating: The fact that you have enemies shooting directly at you, instead of at some soldier on the screen, makes this a far different challenge than *Rush 'N Attack* or *Commando.*

The addition of the innocent bystanders makes it even more challenging.

Challenge: B+

Graphics: B— (the animation could be better)

Sound Effects: B— (nothing spectacular)

CHAPTER TWENTY-ONE

PAPERBOY

Type: Dangerous newspaper route.

Objective: As you pedal your bike through suburbia, you must toss your tabloid into subscribers' Mailboxes . . . while simultaneously avoiding the many dangers on the sidewalks and streets.

Layout: The screen scrolls diagonally, from top right to bottom left. The Training Course scrolls in the same direction (see Training Tips).

Hero: Your news carrier has the ability to toss Papers and to bike—which includes the power to accelerate and brake, and also to shift directions. There are only a limited number of Papers in the bag, however, and these must be replenished by grabbing Bundles, which appear *at random* throughout the ride. Note: You can stop an approaching Dog or Tire dead in its tracks by hitting them with a Newspaper. You won't get points, just a moment's peace of mind!

Enemies: The obstacles are listed in the instruction booklet. Many are also discussed below.

Menu: There are one- or two-player games.

Scoring: You earn points for hitting subscriber Mailboxes or Stoops, or using your Newspapers to break the windows of people who don't subscribe, knocking over Garbage Cans, Bushes, and other items listed in the instructions. Delivering every Paper on your route inspires households that canceled their subscriptions to resubscribe.

Beginner's Strategy: As in real life, there is no pattern to the order in which obstacles appear. For example, although the Tire comes first and the Mower second *most* of the time on Monday, Skateboard Fiends have been known to zoom right at you. (A note about the Tires: On Monday, they always come at you, then swerve to roll down the street. They don't get pushy until Tuesday.) And a word about biking: Although the Sidewalk is the best place to travel, don't hesitate to go up on the Driveways and Lawns. For one thing, the all-important Bundles usually appear in these places. For another, while there are Trees and Fences up here, which you must maneuver around, these are stationary items! It's easier to brake and squeeze through two of these than to have to dodge a moving Dog and a Tornado! (Incidentally, it's a good idea to slow down and be ready to bop the Dogs. If Bundles appear while they're chasing you, the canines will doggedly remain between you, keeping you from fresh Papers!) Speaking of Tornadoes, which usually start after you on Tuesdays: When you see one forming to your right, hit the pedals and speed away!

When it comes to hitting Mailboxes, obviously a lot depends upon where you are and at what speed you're traveling. For instance, if you're on the sidewalk and going top speed, release your Paper when you're at the line in the pavement just below the Mailbox you want to hit. If you want to hit a Tombstone from the same location and at the same speed, fling your Paper when you are *directly* beside it. Regardless of your speed and location, there's one thing you can do: If it looks as if you overthrew the target, *brake!* You'll slow the scrolling of the screen down, but not the speed of your Paper. If you do this carefully, you can make adjustments in the trajectory of the tossed tabloid!

A word about getting through the cross streets. Motorcycles come at you here, starting in pairs. If one has just passed, race across, and the second will miss you. If one comes racing at you when you're in mid-crossing, you are *usually* better off speeding across instead of braking. Braking actually gives the Motorcycle more of a target—your front, middle, and end—whereas a mad dash usually leaves just your tail vulnerable! Also, be aware that Motorcycles start coming in groups of four on Wednesday.

A final warning: Although you can ride on the Curb, beware of Grates. These will knock you down, even up here!

Advanced Strategy: If you're an ambitious player, try the Street delivery route. You can squeeze around the green Cars to the right, around the red Cars to the left, and brake and/or get up on the Sidewalk to avoid Manholes. This isn't easy, but the great thing about the Street is how simple it is to hit objects with Papers! Simply keep your hand off the controller/joystick (in other words, leaving the controller at rest in the middle), thus allowing your carrier to move at a steady pace (though you have to keep your hand above it, prepared to brake or swerve if a Car or Street obstacle appears, or to race to the left when a Bundle appears). When you see a target on the left that you want to hit, just toss your Paper when you're even with it. The tabloid is certain to go in!

Par: Most adequate players can get through Wednesday, with an average of 10,000 points per day, and another 4000 in the Training Course.

Training Tips: Thoughtfully, *Paperboy* has a Training Course to which you go after you finish your route. This really buffs your skills to a high gloss! Avoid the ramps, here, if your interest is solely on training (how many ramps do you face on your route?). Concentrate on tossing Papers into the hoops and steering around obstacles. It's also a good idea to run through the first level, just practicing your biking now and then. If that's second nature, and you can concentrate on your Paper flinging, you'll go far in the business!

Rating: *Paperboy* is unlike anything else on the

market. Although it *seems* to be tame, it requires great dexterity to master. The only drawback: There isn't anything really spectacular to look at as you play (even the Grim Reaper is bland), though the sound effects are exceptional!

Challenge: B+
Graphics: C+
Sound: A

CHAPTER TWENTY-TWO

RAMPAGE

Type: Destruction of cities.

Objective: It's about time: *You're* the baddie! As a giant monster, you roam the United States punching out Buildings, pulverizing Helicopters, chowing down on People, and destroying cities.

Layout: The screen doesn't scroll. There are 128 cities in all; each is represented by a stationary screen showing one or more Buildings and their meager military defenses. There's also a Map Screen that shows how much of the U.S. you've successfully obliterated.

Hero: The player is either the titanic George the Ape or Lizzie the Lizard. As such, you have the ability to jump, climb Buildings, and punch. George is a better climber; Lizzie is fleeter. Both monsters can also eat, which they must do to keep their Energy up. Important note: If you're playing against each other, you can eat your foe when she/he reverts to human form.

Enemies: The instruction booklet describes the Soldiers, Vehicles, Lightning, and Photographers (with their blinding flashes!) who can hurt you. Note: The booklet also lists objects that you *shouldn't* consume.

Menu: One player can enjoy the game alone, or two can partake in the devastation simultaneously. The players can work together to destroy a city . . . or (and this is the most fun of all!) against one another.

Scoring: You earn points for the havoc you wreak. You also gain Energy by eating good things, lose it for consuming bad things, and also lose it when you're hurt by foes (see Enemies). Keep in mind that when your monster dies, though you continue the game from where you were, all your points go down the drain.

Beginner's Strategy: The basic rule is, when you're climbing two or three Buildings that overlap, don't just concentrate on one Building. Whack left, right, center, and so on as you climb. You'll do more destruction in a shorter amount of time and suffer less damage to your monstrous person. Also, if you want to cheat a little, when you start to transform back into a person, keep pressing the B button—you'll stay a monster, *and* you'll keep your points.

Advanced Strategy: Battling another player with the city as your arena requires certain skills. For one, when you punch the other monster near either side of the screen, they will go flying off that side and into the other side. However, you can't chase them. Thus, you have to turn around and cross the screen to get at them again. This will give them time to recover. Also, if your foe is on top of a Building, work furiously to knock it down; the other monster will fall, become dazed, and be a more vulnerable target. If your opponent dies, a new monster will be dropped in by dirigible; bash it in the head while it's descending. This will leave them reeling. Also, don't overlook the value of getting on top of a Building yourself and leaping off onto a foe. Obviously, you have to do this before your adversary knocks the Building down. But if you employ this maneuver successfully, landing on her or his head, you'll leave them with a whopper of a headache.

Par: You should earn an average of 12,500 points per city in a one-player game. Two-player, obviously, depends upon how good your opponent is!

Training Tips: Bash. Just bash. Use the one player mode and practice moving your monster around so that this is second nature when you fight another player for monster supremacy.

Rating: A very good adaptation of the arcade game, with unusual and entertaining gameplay!

Challenge: B— (one-player), A (two-player)
Graphics: A—
Sound: B

CHAPTER TWENTY-THREE

R.C. PRO AM

Type: Car race.

Objective: Speeding around a series of tracks, you must outrace three Drone opponents, collecting weapons all the while and surviving increasingly treacherous road surfaces.

Layout: Each track differs, though they are always the same every time you play the game. The objects you pick up or avoid are always in the same places on the different tracks.

Hero: You drive three different cars, each increasingly fleeter; as you reach various plateaus, you move up to one of the better cars. You have the ability to regenerate quickly after a crash, and to bump into other cars, causing them to be totaled. (If they collide with the wreck of your car, they'll also be fodder for the scrap heap.) The best kind of bumping is against an opponent who is gaining on you. It's easy to whomp them with your rear fender; just sidle over to where they are and do it. You won't even break your stride!

The instruction booklet details the Bombs, Ammo, and other items you can gather. Several of these are also discussed below. Note: You can't shoot your opponents when they're off the screen. You must see them to hit them.

Enemies: Your three Drone foes also get faster and pushier as the game progresses. After a crash, each opponent is back on the road in two seconds. The booklet tells about the road hazards you'll face; many are discussed below.

Menu: There is only a one-player game.

Scoring: You earn points for winning, placing, or showing. Come in "out" (fourth) three times, and the game's over. What's more, you can't continue the game from where you ran your last losing race! Collecting Bonus Letters on the track and spelling "Nintendo" will earn you 40,000 points and a faster car.

Beginner's Strategy: At the onset, a word of warning: If you're in last place during a race, you may be tempted to stop, wait for your enemies to come up behind you on their next lap, and then bomb them. Don't. You can't possibly make up the time you lost waiting for them in the time it takes them to regenerate after being blown up. Another word of warning: If you have the Advantage, don't use Turbo. You'll stand still.

A general rule: Keep an eye on the overview screen at the bottom. If one or even two cars are way ahead of you, concentrate on holding the course and coming in third. Better that, and being able to continue, than to try and race ahead, crash, and watch dumbly as the last car passes you! Having said that, if the fourth car is close on your tail, it pays to gamble and try to bump or shoot it. The two seconds you gain while it's destroyed can make all the difference.

Here is a brief overview of the first ten courses, and the number or laps (in parentheses):

1. (two) Nothing extraordinary here. Just learn to take the turns with your rear tires swinging into them. That's the best way to hold them.

2. (two) There are Missiles here. Watch for them and grab them. You don't have to use them—they'll stay with your car into subsequent races.

3. (three) Watch for the first of the Zippers on this course. Those are red hatch marks that work like afterburners and really speed you up!

4. (two) Your Drone adversaries are a little more persistent. If you can't use your rear to knock them away, you can safely do so with your nose. Especially in the turns (they'll go flying off the road).

5. (three) You'll be pestered by Rain Squalls here; these aren't too difficult to maneuver around or even through, if you must.

6. (four) Stay inside for the first Zipper, then shoot to the outside for four in a row! Don't be afraid to take them—there are no curves in your immediate future.

7. (three) This is a curvy rat of a track, so be

prepared to do most of your racing with the nose of the car pointing inside, so you don't go spinning off in turns.

8. (four) When you hit the straightaway near the end of the first lap, there are six Missiles on each side! Take one side on one lap, then the other side next lap. Note: It'll help to ride the guardrail in order to line up and collect them.

9. (four) All four Zippers are on the outside. If you've been used to speeds of the 90 mile-per-hour sort, you're going to be surprised by your eighties here.

10. (two) There are Puddles galore here—first water, then Oil Slicks. The water isn't so bad, but if you hit the oil, you'll spinout for sure.

Advanced Strategy: Here is an overview of courses eleven through twenty-two:

11. (three) The game speeds you up here with a faster car (whether you want one or not!). Brace yourself for a 120 mile-per-hour race!

12. (five) There're a lot of Oil Slicks, but there's also a nice clear straightaway near the beginning to let you build up a good lead.

13. (three) Pretty easy, with tight turns at the beginning and end, but two very long straightaways top and bottom.

14. (two) Lots of Oil Slicks here; go into the first turn very slowly.

15. (four) You get tons of Missiles here; they're literally everywhere. Stay in the low

eighties to grab them, and rely on bumping rather than speed to beat your opponents.

16. (five) Skip the Zippers on the first lap. Stay inside and get the Missiles. You'll need the Zippers in later laps for speed.

17. (three) Another fast course! Watch out for the Skulls, which crop up here and steal from your arsenal. There are some very useful Zippers on the big curve at the top of the course.

18. (two) A superfast course, and slippery! You'll be lucky to do faster than the seventies here.

19. (four) The Pop-up Barriers emerge here, and you'll learn to hate these. There's one on the bottom, one on top, and they'll leave your car a crumpled mess.

20. (three) Again, you'll find a plethora of Missiles here.

21. (six) The two Zippers on the right side (the part of the track that heads down) are going to prove very important to victory.

22. (five) Your Drone adversaries are extremely fast and aggressive here. Make sure you get a good kick from the Zippers on the top straightaway.

Par: Things don't really get tough until the eighteenth lap. Most players amass 20,000 points in the first five races and 60,000 by twenty. First-place finishes become rarer after that, so scores will vary widely.

Training Tips: As you run through the laps, practicing your driving, don't bother trying to stay precisely on the road at the expense of speed (with rare exceptions, as on course 14, described above). It's okay to skid off; better to lose time here than to take it too cautiously. Practice getting back on the road after hitting the grass.

Rating: I prefer *Spy Hunter* and *Rad Racer,* because you can really build up a head of steam racing in those games. The turns come too quickly for you to get any real momentum going in *R.C. Pro Am.* But the bumping, shooting, and sharp curves here are more than enough to satisfy any driving-game fanatic.

Challenge: B
Graphics: B
Sound: B

CHAPTER TWENTY-FOUR

RING KING

Type: Boxing match.

Objective: To beat a variety of opponents and thus rise in your own abilities.

Layout: The screen shows a Boxing Ring, and scrolls around in response to how the combatants move. The game allows you to play in a training mode or in three progressively more difficult rankings.

Hero: You're a novice Boxer, and as you work your way through the rankings, your endurance (that is, Power Points) increases. You have the ability to throw a variety of punches with the A button (the basic Hook, Uppercut, Straight Punch, and Body Blow—which is basically a Straight Punch thrown at a crouch— as well as varieties thereof, depending upon your Power Points and whether or not your opponent's defenses are up); you defend yourself with the B button, the game automatically dishing up whatever defense is appropriate to the moment.

Enemies: As you progress through the rankings, the skills of your foes also increase. See instruction booklet for details.

Menu: There are one- and two-player games.

Scoring: You box for Power Points, successful maneuvers and victories enabling you to become stronger. Passwords allow you to start new games with previously acquired Points.

Beginner's Strategy: The way to win bouts is to master the counterpunch. When your adversary throws something at you, his guard will be down; the ideal situation is to be able to duck a blow, thus staying in close enough to hit back. Thus, your foe weakens from both his own missed punch and your sock to the gut.

One important thing to watch out for: During a bout, some benevolent member of the crowd may toss a P into the Ring. If you can get over and grab it, you'll boost your Power Points—even if you lose the fight!

By the way, if you can work your opponent over to the Ropes, have a lot of Power Points, and land a good, solid Uppercut, you can knock your adversary out of the ring and into another cartridge!

One more thing: If you knock an opponent off his feet using a powerful Uppercut, he'll do a half somersault and plummet toward the canvas headfirst. Try bashing him again and see what happens.

Advanced Strategy: Had enough punishment? Here's a way to make yourself as invincible as Superman! Make sure both controllers are plugged in. When the Training Gym screen appears, listing everyone's abilities, punch the following buttons in this sequence (C-1 stands for Controller One, C-2 for—you guessed it!—Controller Two): C-2 A button; C-1 A, Select, A; C-2 B; C-1 Select: C-2 A, B; C-1 B, B. That's it! Not even Ali could whup you now!

Par: An average Boxer should be able to win at the U.S. 3 level.

Training Tips: This one's obvious: Stay in the training mode until you're ready to take on the pros!

Rating: This one's not quite as flamboyant as Mike Tyson's game, but it's very good . . . especially when the thrill of *Mike Tyson's Punch-Out* has worn off!

Challenge: B

Graphics: B

Sound: B+

CHAPTER TWENTY-FIVE

RYGAR

Type: Fantasy quest.

Objective: Ensconced in his flying castle, Ligar descends upon the peaceful kingdom of Argool and, with his murderous minions, conquers the citizenry and deposes the Indora Gods. He also takes away the Door to Peace, the symbol of Argool's erstwhile contentment. The Argoolians pray for a savior, and from the land of Algosu comes Rygar to pit his might against that of Ligar.

Layout: The screen scrolls both horizontally and vertically

Hero: The fresh-from-the-box Rygar can walk, crouch, leap, climb, and fire a swirling Diskarmer which shoots out from his wrist like a yo-yo blade. Along the way he can obtain Physical Strength Units (small ewers), a Wind Pulley for crossing crevasses, a Grappling Hook for vertical climbs, a Crossbow (for climbing at angles), a Suit of Armor, a Coat of Arms (allows instant healing), the Flute of

Pegasus (opens an important doorway and is
not well-liked by Ligar), and Capsules (which
look like stones with stars) that increase Spir-
itual Strength (listed on the game's sub-
screen): Power-Up (allows the Grappling
Hook to be extended even farther), Attack &
Assail (hurts your foes), and Recover (restores
physical strength). These boons come either
from Hermits or remain behind when enemies are slain.

Enemies: There are numerous monsters that
plague Rygar's way.

Menu: There is only the one-player game. Upon
death, it can be continued from the beginning
of the last level.

Scoring: The only measure of Rygar's accom-
plishments is how much weaponry and
strength he collects.

Beginner's Strategy: We are going to concentrate,
here, on the routes through every realm to final victory. Along the way you will be set-
upon by monsters; these must be dealt with by
squatting and firing, by leaping over them, or
in some cases (as with Pragokelis) by jumping
on top of them. We'll detail only a few key kill-
ings, some of the tougher monsters as well as
the "Stage Bosses"—the beasts that guard captured Indora Gods.

To begin: Go right to the first Rope, climb,
head right to the second Rope, climb. Enter
the column and consult with the God, if you
wish. Exit, staying on the column, go right to
the next post (to avoid the pit below), then
down. Head right to the third Rope on the bot-

tom, then turn left, back to the Door on the second level (for our purposes, Door One). *This Door is an important landmark, so note its location.* (Note: If you go to the second level earlier, you'll run smack into that big stone wall to the left of the Door.) Enter, and you're in the Valley of Garloz. Note where this Door—Door Two—is as well! To get the Grappling Hook, go up, left, up, right, and into the Door on the right. Obtain the weapon, then head for the Door that leads to the Rolsa Valley. Go back to Door Two; don't enter, but go up, right, up (past the Rope, which you can't cross because you don't have the Wind Pulley), right, down, right, then up. Climb the steps and enter the Door (hereafter, Door Three). Proceed to the third tower on the right and ascend using the Grappling Hook. Get off on the bridge, go to the right side of the tower, cross to the second tower, and climb the Rope down (otherwise, you won't get across the water). Note: Stop in the rooms up there if you want, but we'll be giving you all the directions here! Back down, head to the next column on the right, ascend with Rope and Grappling Hook, jump along the top, then go down and into the Door. You're now in the Forest of Eruga, the first Stage Boss. Go right to the Ropes, climb, grapple up the tree to the left; the room up there lets you regain your strength. Head right, then down the first Rope. The most dangerous forest denizens you'll face are the Kinatarnos, and there's an easy way to deal with them: When one appears, go back to the left until it's off the screen on the right, then go right again. Most of the time, the monster will vanish! (But beware: Repeat the trick, and the creature will return.) After defeating the first one, get to where the monster was and climb. Go right, into the room, to learn about the two-headed fire-breathing turtle bear Eruga. Go right, down the Rope, and right to the Door to face Eruga. Attack & Assail is necessary here, and there are three ways of battling the monster: jump over the flame, fire into its face, leap to avoid its flame. Repeat. You can also perform this strategy from the safety of the ledge on the left, jumping down, firing, jumping back, jumping down again, etc. However, the coolest way to kill the monster is this: Leap to the monster's right side and face left. Shoot it, leap onto its head when it fires its beams at you (you're still facing left), hop back to the right (still facing the monster), shoot into its face, and repeat. This is the fastest way, and it also requires the most skill. In any case, the monster is now history. The Door to the right of Eruga's lair provides you with the Wind Pulley.

Leave and go up, right, and up. Enter the Door there for strength. Now, hitch up your trousers for a hike. Go down, left, down, left, and down to the Rope. Cross using the Wind Pulley, then go down and left to the next Rope. Cross and go left, up, left, down, left, up, and left to the Door. This leads to the Mountain Primeval. Hurry through the door to the right, leaping the pit to avoid the Pragokelis on the left. Cross two Ropes and go right, not ever stopping, just shooting the oncoming monsters as you go. When you reach a door, enter; keep going right through the cavern, across a Rope, to the Door. Head left, go down the Rope, continue to the left, grapple down at the Platform (the circular stone over a pit), go left to the end of the ledge, grapple down again, and go left. Again, at the end of the ledge, grapple down. Now, head right to the Door. Inside, you'll find Sagila, the spider. The Stage Boss is easy to slay; shoot Sagila. This will bring it scuttling toward you, up the wall, along the ceiling, and down the other side. As it does so, you shift to the other side. As soon as Sagila reaches the bottom of the wall opposite you, blast it. It will then come after you the same way; you shift sides again, shoot, and repeat until the arachnid's a goner. Get the Crossbow from the Door on the right. Head left, down, left, up, and pass the Door on the right (again, you'll learn the same news in this book, a bit later on). Continue up, then right to the Tree Stump. Use your Crossbow and Power-Up to get to the island. Enter the door there. (Note: There's another door, in the water above the island. Explore that one on your own time . . . we've got to leave some secrets!)

On the other side of the door is a maze. Go right, up and over the pit, right, and up. Ignore the door. Head up, jump the pit, go up, left, and down. Use your Crossbow at the

Stump. (The Door there tells you you're halfway through!) Go left, up, and into the door for news about Dorago and the speaker's daughter. Then go down, left, up, right, down the left side of the columns, then back up the center, shooting and/or jumping the monsters. When you come to the door, enter to face Dorago, the red demon.

Advanced Strategy: Beat Dorago by jumping from side to side in front of the creature, avoiding its flameballs while shooting back. Make sure you employ both Attack & Assail and, to ensure victory (though this isn't absolutely necessary), access your own recovery powers. After Dorago perishes, enter the door and get the Coat of Arms. Return through the maze to the small island. From there, retrace your steps to Door Two. (Again, don't go in: This is just your general landmark.) Head up and right, then up to the Rope, cross, continue right, move up and right, then down and right, and keep going right to the Door. Enter, and you're on the floating island Lapis.

Go right and up the first Rope. Enter the Door and head right, go up the Rope and jump the pit. At the ledge fire the Grappling Hook straight into the air; it will catch a ledge up there. When you ascend, go up and get your footing fast; a Super-robot (Bargan) will drop down, spitting its crescent rays. Jump the rays and blast the monster. Ignore the Door when you continue. At the Stump fire your Crossbow at an angle to the right, shimmy across to the sky ledge, then repeat down to the right. Jump the small ledges and bypass the Door. Grapple down from the tip of the right side, then Crossbow down to the left. Go left, stopping at the fat boulder on the far left. Grapple down, use your Wind Pulley to go right, then continue to the right, blasting the falling Superrobots as you go. (If you need a breather, attach your Grappling Hook to a ledge and lower yourself down. Just hang there until you're ready to continue.)

When you reach the door, enter for the message if you wish, then exit, use the Grappling Hook to descend, then take the Wind Pulley to the left. Ignore the green area; stay on the platforms. Keep going left and enter the Door. When you go in, quickly grapple up to the monster's ledge and shoot it before it turns. It gives up the ghost without much of a struggle. Behind the door to the left is the Coat of Armor. Now comes a long retracing of your steps. Go back to Door Two, which leads to Door One (the Door to the right of that big, fat wall at the beginning). Once there, go right, up the Rope, left, up the Rope, left, jump the pit, and continue left. Climb the Rope and grapple up two levels to the door on top; get the Coat of Arms, if you wish. If not, go right, past the next door, to the Rope. Cross, continue right to the next Rope, cross again, cross using the third Rope, then enter the door on the right. This leads to the Tower of Garba. Kill the Kuzeelar you'll probably find there, climb the Rope, do some killing in the next room, head left, climb the Rope, then go right.

Fight or jump the monster, go up the last Rope, and voilà! You're face to ugly face with the Demorobruzer. Deal with it as you dealt with Sagila, the spider. (Having the Coat of Arms is a help in this bout.) Go in the door and obtain the all-important Pegasus Flute.

With the Flute in hand, return to Door One. Take it to Door Two and head to Door Three. Entering, go right, to the second tower. Climb, go right, jump past the door, and continue right to the third tower. Use the Grappling Hook to climb. (Note: When there are no more ledges on which to grapple, you'll have to switch to the right side of the tower. In short order, on the upper right, you'll spot the lion-headed mouth of Ligar's Castle. Toot your Flute and a Door will appear. Climb to it and take the route described below, shooting the Shadow Monsters as you go (Note: Since the view is overhead now, the direction "up" means to go straight ahead; it does not mean to ascend); head right, up, and left through the Arch into the Castle proper. Go through the Arches in the rooms as follows: up, upper left, bottom right. Note this point (Arch One) if you wish to take a side trip to get a Coat of Arms. If you do, head through rooms by going down, down, and right. Get the Coat and return to Arch One. Go left, down, cross the two pits, and right through the Arch. Go right, right, down, left through the columns, into the Arch on the left, travel up, cross the pit, continue through two Arches, go right, then cross the ether using the Stumps. Enter the sanctum of Ligar. Fight using Attack & Assail, Recover, and it wouldn't hurt to blow the Flute (the villain's snake arms don't care for it much). If you fail in your efforts to best the fiend, go back through the Castle, killing monsters and obtaining potions, then return for another tilt with the beast.

Par: There are really three skill landmarks: A so-so player will be stymied by Eruga; a good player will get as far as Dorago; and, of course, an excellent player will go all the way to Ligar.

Training Tips: Most importantly, make a map. You'll need this in case you die during play. Secondly: Be certain you know how to jump with skill and precision. In some cases this skill is more important than your Diskarmer; for example, in the very early stages when Pragokelises swarm at you and you don't feel like stopping to kill them all. Finally, experiment and be familiar with all the weapons and restorative powers at your disposal. Know which to use when, and how to get to them quickly on the sub-screen.

Rating: As quests go, this game is pretty pedestrian. It's not as complex as *Wizards & Warriors,* nor is the shooting as quick as in *Gauntlet.* The scenery's quite handsome, however, and the colors and animation are also fine.

Challenge: C+

Graphics: B+

Sound: C+

CHAPTER TWENTY-SIX

SECTION Z.

Type: Outer space search-and-destroy.

Objective: In the twenty-first century earth's Saturn Space Station sends a warning about an invasion . . . and then communications stop. As Captain Commando, you must fly into space and battle the imperious Space Soldiers of Balangool, fighting all the way to Balangool's Master Control, the L-Brain, located in Section Z of the enemy defenses.

Layout: The screen scrolls horizontally as you fight your way through four different levels, each of which contains many corridors and rooms (there are a total of sixty chambers!) which you must clear of invaders. Rooms are accessed by reaching the end of another room; there, you enter a beam and are warped to another chamber.

Hero: Captain Commando has the ability to walk, fly, and shoot backward or forward. As Captain Commando gains ground, he can

Power-Up with various weapons (described in the instruction booklet, and also below).

Enemies: There are twenty different mobile space adversaries, all of whom are discussed in the booklet (and many below). You also must face stationary Turrets.

Menu: There is just the one-player game.

Scoring: You earn points for shooting alien armaments, from 60 for a Crowd Eye to 120 for a Turret, 240 for a Crab, and so on as you progress. You also lose an Energy point when you're hit by a bullet; you lose a life when struck by an enemy vessel.

Beginner's Strategy: Here are the general ways with which to deal with the creatures and machines you'll meet in the first phase of play.

Room One: Beat the Crowd Eyes by hitting the left column first (so the bonuses don't scroll off the left side of the screen when you move right). Then stay to the top and shoot the Turret there; remain on top, firing continuously, to pick off the Gromas that arrive, then slip to the bottom and blast the Gromas there. From One you can go up to Two or down to Three.

Room Two: Go immediately to the top; take out the Turret there, then go right and through the room quickly; a Missiledrone will sneak up behind you! Fight your way through, roughly beneath your score, halfway down. From Two you can go down to Three or up to Four.

Room Three: Go to the bottom, halfway

across, and shoot while you walk. A Crab will arrive within moments. Then hurry to the upper right, face left, and blast the Crab which will be behind you . . . but coming up fast! If you aren't fast enough to kill it, simply (and easily) dodge its bullets while moving right. If the Transporter isn't active when you arrive, seek sanctuary behind it, to the right. The Crab's bullets can't reach you there. Move into the Transporter when it glows; down will take you to Four, up to Six.

Room Four: Same as Room One, as far as the Crowd Eyes go. When the Leagos arrive, get to the right and shoot left; if you don't get them, they'll sweep over and charge at you from that direction. After three waves, go left and then right to face the last enemies. Note: Take the bullet hits rather than touch the Leagos. From Four you can go up to Six or down to One (you get to Five by going up from Six).

Room Five: Turn at once for an attack from behind, then go to the right and fight the Leagos. Go down to get to Room Eight from here, or up to Seven.

Room Six: Stay to the bottom to start and shoot the Missiledrones (ducking into the niches there when necessary). Pick your way slowly to the top, in a diagonal movement toward the upper right. Get the Turret there.

Other rooms are described below.

Advanced Strategy: The map of the remainder of the rest of the first third of the complex is as follows: Take Eight up to Five, down to

Eleven; Eleven up to Nine, down to Ten; Ten up to Eight, down to Nine; Nine both ways to Six. Six, bottom, leads to Twelve; Twelve up goes to Thirteen, down to Fourteen; Thirteen and Fourteen both go up to Sixteen, down to Eighteen; Sixteen heads up to Fifteen, down to Eighteen; Eighteen takes you up to Sixteen, down to Seventeen; Seventeen only goes to Nineteen; Nineteen just leads to Twenty; Twenty spirits you down to Twenty-one and up to Twenty-two.

There are Transmitters you must destroy. These are located in Six, Eighteen, Twenty-one, Twenty-two, Forty-three, and Fifty-seven. To get to them, however, you must shut down the impenetrable barriers that protect them. The Generators powering these are to be found in Eleven, Sixteen, Twenty-nine, Thirty-four, Forty-nine, and Fifty-six.

You'll have to fight Bosses in Nineteen and Thirty-two (Zamusa), Thirty-Nine and Fifty-two (Balaba), and Forty-five (Galga).

As for Power-Up super weapons, you will find the following weapons in the sections listed:

Megasmasher: Two, Ten, Thirteen, Thirty-five, Forty-one, Forty-six. Flash Buster: Four, Eight, Twenty, Thirty-seven, Forty-four, Fifty-four. Barrier Shield: Seven, Eight, Nine, Seventeen, Twenty-two, Forty-two, Fifty-five, and Forty-eight. Metal Eater: Twelve and Twenty-eight. And a Crush Ball in Twenty-One. As for Energy Tubes to keep you fit and flying, they're in Nine (top), Fourteen (bottom),

Twenty-eight (top), Thirty-five (top), Thirty-six (top), Forty-one (bottom), and Fifty-three (bottom). The other Power-Up items are comparatively plentiful.

Par: A good player will get as far as destroying the second Generator/Transmitter combo. Points vary widely, since players take different routes through the space czar's sanctuary.

Training Tips: Practice maneuvering your space ace—preferably in Six, where Missiledrones come at you thick and furious (like Weapons 'R Us had a clearance sale and L-Brain went and bought up the inventory). Don't rely just on your shooting ability—that alone won't enable you to make it all the way through!

Rating: A fast-moving game with the added challenge of the maze layout; you don't just shoot your way ahead, you have to know where everything leads!

Challenge: A—

Graphics: A

Sound: B

CHAPTER TWENTY-SEVEN

SEICROSS

Type: Motorcycle obstacle course.

Objective: On the distant world Colura the peaceful Petras have been attacked and driven underground by the wicked Basrah tribe. However, a few Petras remained above ground . . . prey for the Basrah! Thus, they cobbled together a motorbike known as Gilgitt Petras and sent it forth to collect the stragglers.

Layout: The game scrolls from right to left, and displays the bizarre weapons and landmarks of the surface of Colura.

Hero: On board your Gilgitt Petras you race across the surface of Colura, shooting the enemy while scooping up Petras. You have the ability to maneuver to the top or the bottom of the screen or play anywhere from the left side of the screen to the right as the terrain flashes by. Important note: Watch for Stars when you destroy things. You get extra points . . . except for the Stars that come from Radar

Buoys. These boost your firepower from a measly one to a whopping *nine* scatter bullets everytime you pull the trigger!

Enemies: The instruction booklet details twenty different kinds of foes you will encounter. However, a note about the Powarmons: If you're in a tight spot when these appear, you don't have to hit both terminals to deactivate the electrical arc. Just shoot one. You won't get the points, but you won't get electrocuted either.

Menu: Two players can race in their own, alternating matches.

Scoring: You obtain points for saving Petras and for killing Basrah and destroying their armaments. (The point values are listed in the instructions.) You must also collect Energy Packs to keep your tank from running dry (each Pack replenishes one quarter of your supply, or three of the twelve-unit capacity). You cannot store more than your tank's limit.

Beginner's Strategy: A general suggestion: Try to race in loops. That is, stay one third to one half of the way in from the left, and as enemy bikes shoot in, be prepared to swing down and all the way to the left in a clockwise direction, or up and far left counterclockwise. This will allow you to see the bikes coming in from the left, and enable you to blast them. At the same time, playing more than halfway to the right is usually risky in this game, as it doesn't give you time to react to whatever obstacles are sweeping in from that side. (Note: Although you *can* bump Basrah bikes aside, you don't get any points unless they total themselves by crashing into a wall, top or bottom. Also, bumping is only a temporary solution to the problem.) Speaking of the top and bottom walls, *you* can crash into them without being destroyed, though it costs you energy.

When obstacles come at you too quickly and you can't make the looping moves, the best tack is to stay in the vertical middle behind a spray of gunfire. This will leave you well-positioned to dart up or down to confront (or avoid!) whatever foe comes at you.

Finally, one of the quirks of the game you should be aware of: The game moves quicker on the odd screens.

Advanced Strategy: Here are two nifty tips. When you reach the end of one level, you'll come to a START sign. The instant the game begins, shoot to the top of the screen; you can gather a goodly number of the Petras standing there. Also, if you've been defeated and don't want to go back to the beginning, simply wait until the title screen comes on, hold down the A button, and press Start. The game will resume on the level you left off. (Don't be greedy, though: This usually won't work more than three times in succession.)

A few words about dealing with three pesky foes. In order to beat the BalTanks, you're going to have to get off a lot of hits . . . while they're shooting at you. These enemies move up and down; go in the same direction they are, just slightly ahead of them. (In other words, if they're going up, you go up too—

slightly higher than they are.) This will allow you to get your shots in without being hit. The other troublesome foes are the Aptons and Warme Stones. These can wreck you even after they're beaten, since the husks remain. However, if you've got guts, keep shooting at them: As long as you're willing to play chicken, they're willing to feed you points!

One last thing: If you want to get yourself a super-cycle, here's how. When the title screen appears, use the second controller as follows: hold down the A and B buttons while pressing the joystick left. At the same time, have someone push up, up, down, down, and Start on the first controller.

Par: A good player should collect 60,000 points for each level of play.

Training Tips: Practice maneuvering through the various levels of play *without* firing. If you can go far with just weaving and bumping, imagine how well you'll do when you bring your guns into play!

Rating: There is nothing here you haven't seen in games like *Excitebike*—though it's never been done quite so surreal, colorful, or fast-paced!

Challenge: B
Graphics: B
Sound: C

CHAPTER TWENTY-EIGHT

SUPERMAN

Type: Fantasy quest.

Objective: As you walk, leap, and fly through Metropolis, you endeavor to find and defeat various crime bosses until you meet the chief evil genius, Lex Luthor.

Layout: The game scrolls primarily side to side, with occasional vertical flight. There's also a (terrific!) screen, which is a bird's-eye view from above Superman, looking down at the city (this repeats whenever he is flying from place to place). The game also offers a map mode, so you can chart your course.

Hero: Superman, the superhero from the planet Krypton, is somewhat different from his comic-book and motion-picture counterpart: He can't use the bulk of his powers unless he collects Blue Power Crystals and Power Icons along the way (he beats them out of enemies). These run dry quickly and must constantly be replenished. Also, Superman can only use one power at a time. As for vulnerabilities, he can be weakened by Red Kryptonite, and his powers diminished even more by Green Kryptonite. These, too, pop out of enemies, and are especially dangerous because they resemble Blue Power Crystals. The only powers Superman has at the beginning are a powerful punch, the ability to leap (though not over tall buildings; he has to fly), and hovering ability, which is the not-so-great power to float down slowly after a jump. Note: You can do a "double-hover" when you leap off an awning, phone booth, steps, or other elevated object. Leap off the object, and as you descend, hovering, leap again. That'll carry you much farther and is especially useful when you've got wall-to-wall enemies in front of you.

Enemies: There are over twenty different characters, most of whom are detailed in the instruction booklet, and many of whom are discussed below.

Menu: There is only the one single-player game.

Scoring: You gain (and lose) powers as you go, as well as Attack Points and Defense Points, which dictate your levels of endurance.

Beginner's Strategy: Since *Superman* is a game that depends more on searching for clues than on bashing enemies, it would spoil the fun to tell you everything. What follows are a few things you will need to do on various levels. First, some notes. The same Power Icons do not always come from the same enemies . . . though if you travel underground, you'll usually find the Warriors there fessing up a lot of beneficial Icons. Not only that, but these dudes only take two punches to fell—unlike most other foes, who require three or four. Also, as you move through different levels of the game, remember that the same passersby will always tell you the same things. Don't waste time flapping your lips for nothing. And be careful not to hit a bad guy toward the edges of the screen. If the Crystal or Icon flies off the screen, you can't simply zip to the next screen and get it; it's gone. Finally, make a note where all the phone booths and closets are (the latter, for example, in Wonderland Toys and Prescott's Department Store). If you lose too much power and automatically turn back to Clark Kent, you'll need to know where these places are so you can become Superman once again!

On the first level, leave the *Daily Planet* and go right. Become Superman in the phone booth. Your ultimate destination is the Appollo (sic) Theater, which is located over the S in Metropolis Park on the map. Roam around outside, clobbering thugs, until you're fully stocked with Super Powers. Go into the theater, descend—using Super Breath to fight Zoara's minions—then switch to Heat Vision when you get to the bottom. Run under Zoara when she leaps, turn and try to zap her when she lands. Hit her as many times as possible before she breaks out her Whip, which makes her more deadly.

Defeating her, you'll return to the *Daily Planet* and collect the very useful Subway Pass from Jimmy Olsen. The search for the

Dragon will take considerably longer, though here it is in a nutshell: Go from the *Daily Planet* to Mt. Royal. Head left to Glenmorgan Square. Beat up the baddies there, then go to the Stock Market (located to the left of Senneville, where the road bends up). Talk to the brokers inside, and they'll send you to the Fish Market in the Old City. From there you'll be dispatched to One Lexcorp Plaza in Lafayette, where the Dragon's flunkies are supposed to be setting a fire. Once you stop the arsonists, you'll be heading to Teaboro to meet the Dragon. Note: On this level, make sure you chat with the Police.

Advanced Strategy: Strangely, beating the mad Computer is the easiest of all Superman's challenges. Go to Metropolis Park and head left, stopping over the E in Metropolis Park on the map. Enter the Computer Center and go downstairs. (Note: There's a room to the right on the first floor. Skip it. You'll face danger there, just to learn what we're about to tell you!) On the bottom floor, jump up when the Computer isn't firing rays at you, slip into the opening on the Computer's right side, halfway up, and beat the core to bits. That'll stop the menace cold.

What's tougher about this level than all others are the Zombies. You'll meet these fuzzy rats en route. Not only are they tough, they tend to gather in great numbers; you could leap two or three heading left, only to land on one who comes rushing in, headed right. It's better to fight these guys when they appear than to run, since four of them together may prove more than you can handle.

After you've dealt with the Computer, you'll be called upon to rescue a kidnapped professor. Start your quest in Centennial Park, and keep in mind the location of the Police Station!

Here are a few code words to bring you to various advanced levels of gameplay: SUQ KBY HAUD QOB ZMI PU!D will bring you to the level right after the defeat of Zoara; SOA KBY HAUC QOB YYA PUZ' will get you past the Dragon; KVA JBE CQUB IOA HJ? PWEA will take you to the Computer level; and both KKQ JAY CQ(B IOA G?? ?XJV and KCY JAU CQ(B IOA GP? ?X!P will hoist you to stages after the defeat of the Computer (the latter with 440 Attack Points and 220 Defense Points).

Par: A minimal amount of fighting and digging for clues should get you through the Computer level.

Training Tips: The most important thing to remember is to conserve your powers! Thus, learn to use and rely on simple punching. Practice this before you get too deeply into the game and can't afford to lose confrontations. Also, learn to jump and hover! If you're well-stocked with powers, there's no reason to engage in fights with baddies. Learn to jump/hover over two, three, or sometimes four of them, and get on with your mission!

Rating: Fans of *Super Mario Bros.* will enjoy this cartoonish version of the legend, with its hop-and-bop'em gameplay. Also, there's a good deal of challenge in questioning passersby, searching for villains, and traveling to and from different locations in Metropolis. But fans of Superman and/or hard-edged adventure games will be disappointed—the game makers would have been wiser to make this a more realistic seek-and-destroy cartridge.

Challenge: B—

Graphics: C

Sound: B+ (excellent musical score)

CHAPTER TWENTY-NINE

TEENAGE MUTANT NINJA TURTLES

Type: Sword-swinging, bust-'em-up quest.

Objective: You know the pizza-eating heroes from the comics and cartoons—the four turtles who were coated with a strange, glowing liquid and assumed the form of the animal with which they'd most recently been in contact . . . in this case, a ninja. Now they must undermine the power of the evil Shredder and his monstrous Foot Clan by performing several heroic deeds: rescuing the kidnapped April, locating 8 hidden bombs, saving the abducted Master Splinter, penetrating the Technodrome fortress, and finally defeating Shredder.

Layout: The game consists of a series of Areas which scroll primarily from side to side, with occasional vertical moves. There are sub-screen maps which will tell you about each Area's layout, and which scroll in all directions.

Hero: The turtles are Donatello, strong but slow

master of the wooden staff; Michelangelo, expert with the whirling nunchakus, effective against small foes; Raphael, who wields the pronged sai, is fast but has a limited range; and Leonardo, a swordsturtle who is deadly with his katana and also has a heckuva reach! Other weapons you can acquire include a Boomerang, Throwing Stars which can deck more than one enemy at once, Triple Stars (three times as effective as the single Star), a Magic Scroll, and, of course, pizza to restore your turtle's energy levels. There's also the missile-packed "turtlemobile," the Party Wagon. When one turtle is hurt, you have the ability to switch to another in order to prevent the game from ending.

Enemies: In addition to the powerful human Shredder, the turtles will face the tongue-flicking Giant Frog, flame-spitting Fire Freak, the Meka Turtle (a Teen Turtle clone!), Chainsaw Maniac, and many others.

Menu: One player at a time can play.

Scoring: As you play, you build up (or lose) your arsenal and energy. In Area Two, you'll be playing against a timer.

Beginner's Strategy: As you begin the game in Area One, go underground, descend, and head to the right. Climb the second ladder, ascend, cross over to the next platform, jump down, climb the next ladder, jump to the platform to the right, and ascend the ladder there. Cross to the next tunnel, descend, and head right. The door at the end will take you to a building in which you'll find Pizza. (Note: Beware the

Steam Roller when you're outside the tunnels. It's nothing to lose sleep over; just move with a bit of caution.) Before you can climb up and leave the tunnel, you'll meet Rocksteady. Leap, get behind him, and use Donatello to defeat him. Leaving and heading to the left, you'll find another tunnel. Enter and explore, even though it's a dead end. When you get out, you'll find another tunnel entrance in the upper left. If you descend, go left, then leave the tunnel. You'll find a building to the right. Inside are more goodies. April will be on the second floor, to the far left. Guarding her will be the machine-gunning Bibbop. Use Leonardo to defeat him, since that Teen Turtle won't have to get as close to the killer as the others would.

In Area Two, your job is to disarm eight bombs which the villains have planted to destroy a dam . . . and you only have two minutes and twenty seconds to do it! Getting through the three floors inside the dam itself is no problem. The real problem is negotiating the underwater maze, which is where the bombs are. Their locations are as follows:

The first is located to the left of the first mountain on the bottom.

The second is left of the higher, second mountain to the right (immediately after the narrow passage created by the second stalactite you'll encounter).

The third is found midway between these two. Take the channel leading up; the bomb is tucked in the upper left corner.

The fourth is to the right, directly above the spot where you found the second (there are no other landmarks here, so keep a careful eye out).

The fifth is located straight ahead, at the opening of a small niche which points down to the right.

The sixth can be found by going up the channel above the fifth bomb, and following the passageway to the right. It's located at the very end of the channel. You'll pass one tunnel which goes straight down: the bomb is at the top of the second vertical channel (you won't have to go down; the bomb is at the top).

The seventh bomb can be found by doubling back and going down the first vertical channel you saw in this passageway. The channel will fork as you descend: the bomb is in the right fork.

The last bomb can be found by going all the way to the bottom of the underwater area, heading to the right, rising slightly, then going left in a narrow channel.

You're not going to be thrilled with all the enemies you have to face here: deadly Seaweed, strong currents which will carry you off-course, and a few of Shredder's booby-traps. The only way to save yourself from these is by learning to maneuver your Turtle. The important thing is to know where you're going!

Advanced Strategy: Area Three is a tricky, complex region which must be fully explored if the kidnapped Splinter is to be rescued. You'll be using your Party Wagon here to shoot both impasses and enemy vehicles. There are eleven different building entrances or tunnels to enter, and you should try to get to them all. Here's a general directory to what you'll find. If you head to the upper left corner of the screen, you can enter and leave the second building from the left repeatedly in order to collect Pizza for all four Turtles. Missiles are also to be found in this building. Unfortunately, reaching the highest floor here won't be easy. The best way to do it is to stand just to the right of the door on the far left side of the third floor. Jump up, squeezing through the narrow opening above.

Leaving this building, head all the way to the left, then go straight down, then travel to the right all the way to the end, then go down, then turn left. The building here will reward you with Scroll power—a magic beam that will destroy almost anyone who dares to come against you. Leaving and heading back to the top of the complex, if you cross the bridge and go to the building all the way on the top right, you'll find more Scroll power here.

If, along the way, one of the Turtles is taken prisoner, you can find him in a building on the right side of the river. You can locate the building as follows. There's a stone structure which spans the river near the bottom of the screen. The building is the second one above that point, to the right. (The first building you'll see can't be entered.)

You'll find Splinter in the sewers which run

beneath the city. These can be accessed via the building directly above (that is, behind) the building described in the previous paragraph. However, don't go below unless you're well-stocked with Scrolls (50 is a good number; 30 is the minimum, and only if you're a real pro). Don't even dare to go here, however, until you've explored all of the buildings in this Area. Also, from level three on up, you're going to have to jump using a special technique in some tight spots. Use a "feathering" technique, taking mini-jumps by tapping the A button lightly.

Par: A good player will be able to get through the first three levels.

Training Tips: Apart from drawing a map, the key to winning the game is to know your Turtles. Take time to practice with all four, learning their strengths and weaknesses.

Rating: This is one of the few games which is very faithful to its source material *and* lots of fun!
Challenge: B+
Graphics: A
Sound: B

CHAPTER THIRTY

TOWN AND COUNTRY WOOD AND WATER RAGE

Type: Skateboarding and surfboarding madness.

Objective: There are three different contests: Street Skate Session, in which you must skateboard over obstacles to the finish line; Big Wave Encounter, where the challenge is to reach the Beach; and Wood and Water Rage, which dares you to do both in succession.

Layout: The scroll goes from left to right in both games. Obstacles are the same everytime you play, including the non-stationary Balls, Frisbees, etc. in Street Skate Session (Coins are in the same general area as before, though in slightly different locations).

Hero: In Street Skate Session you are either Joe Cool or Tiki Man; for Big Wave Encounter, you can select Thrilla Gorilla or Kool Kat. These provide you with no different skills, though many players swear that Thrilla Gorilla has greater forward momentum because of the simian's enormous bulk.

Enemies: In Street Skate Session there are no living enemies, per se, just obstacles, as detailed in the instruction booklet (along with Bouncing Balls, Crates, Frisbees, and other objects unmentioned). In Big Wave Encounter you face the obstacles mentioned in the booklet, as well as snoozing bathers drifting by on rubber rafts.

Menu: Two players can partake in alternating games. However, both must play the same game.

Scoring: You get points for skillful maneuvers and collecting Coins, and lose Life Points for messing up (Street Skate Session). These are explained in the instruction booklet. What you *aren't* told is that amassing a total of eight Life Symbols will stop the clock! Time remaining at the end of your run is added to the point score. Note: While skateboarding, you get *no* points for hopping onto low-lying Guardrails. Only Street Skate Session is timed. Avoiding obstacles and gathering bananas get you points in Big Wave Encounter, while wipeouts in either game cost you Life Points (and in Street Skate Session also cost you your Coins).

Beginner's Strategy: Keep in mind that when you fall in Street Skate Session you start roughly half a screen back from where you took your spill. You not only lose time, but ground. In Big Wave Encounter inexperienced surfers would do best to rely on the following technique: Keep the controller pressed to the right, quickly and alternately tapping A-B-A-B, etc. This will keep you moving toward the

Beach. If you need to get out of the way of an oncoming obstacle, simply stop pressing the buttons for a second and let the controller alone guide you—but only for a second. Since this technique will keep you relatively close to the bottom of the screen, it may be necessary to make periodic adjustments; to do so, keep the controller pushed right while pushing the B button repeatedly, also just for a second. (Longer, and you'll swing to the left, something you don't really want to do.) If you're a more experienced surfer, what you want to do is surf up and down diagonally (upper left to bottom right, then back to the upper left and repeat). Do this at a steady, rhythmic pace, and you'll cover a little more of the wave each time.

Advanced Strategy: In Street Skate Session a time-saving tactic is to keep the B button depressed when you make your leaps. This enables you to keep up speed when you come down on the other side of the Pit, Sand, etc. Also in this game: On high Guardrails, if you hop on and off and on again, you'll garner extra points for as many times as you can pull the stunt off.

As for Big Wave Encounter, in general you'll be relying more on the B button than on the A in order to avoid the obstacles coming from the right. Here are some additional tips. On screen three, when you use the diagonal maneuver described above, don't come any lower than the white crest in the center of the screen. You'll want to avoid the obstacles below. On screen six, you'll notice that you begin the round with just three surfers (that drops to two on level nine, and a measly one at level twelve). Also on six, the fish and birds come with greater frequency; be ready to ride up to avoid the fish, or to speed down and *stay* down to duck the birds. On seven, a lot of fish will be jumping up at you. On nine, four fish come in rapid succession, followed by a bird. Screen eleven dishes up a lot of bonus bananas. But most important of all, if you want to rack up scores in the hundreds of thousands (yes, you read right: *hundreds* of thousands), instead of just the crummy 20 points for every second you're on your board, all you have to do is spin your surfer in circles at the top of a wave. Move the joystick in a circle (counterclockwise works best), taking one second for each turn. Every time you spin, you'll add 500 points to your score!

Par: You should be able to get 7500 points per level in Street Skate Session and get through each one-minute-timed race in 25 seconds; and get an average of 2000 points for each wave of Big Wave Encounter (unless, of course, you're using the nifty 500 point maneuver, described above.)

Training Tips: Initially, don't worry about points in either game. Go through them to study the courses and obstacles. It's also important, obviously, to master your jumping skills and balance in Street Skate Session and Big Wave Encounter, respectively. Again, go through the early levels worrying about nothing but honing these skills.

Rating: This is a unique and coordination-intensive set of games. Not much thinking involved here, but there's nothing wrong with a cartridge that's just hand-eye skills!
Challenge: A—
Graphics: B+
Sound: B (terrific bird and surf sounds!)

CHAPTER THIRTY-ONE

ZANAC

Type: Futuristic shoot-'em-up.

Objective: Created by unknown aliens to bestow intelligence on those who access its Icons properly, the huge System—a network of rock, metal, and armaments—went haywire. In order to shut down the malfunctioning unit, one pilot must guide the sophisticated AFX-6502-ZANAC through the System's defenses.

Layout: The screen scrolls vertically, though the player has the ability to move from side to side. There are twelve Areas in all, each more dangerous than the one before.

Hero: The stripped-down ZANAC you're handed at the beginning (you get one on screen, two in reserve, and you can earn extras as you go) has conventional Bullets as well as Fire 0—ballistic orbs that can be launched concurrent with Bullets. Power Chips that give you Fire 1 through Fire 7 can be acquired as you go along. These powers are explained in the instruction booklet. Note: Each new Chip you collect supplants the one you were using before it—which isn't necessarily a good thing. What *is* good, though, is the fact that if your ship is destroyed, any Power Chips you'd released will still be floating on the screen when your next ship is delivered. You'll be able to race over and grab it! A few words about some of the Fires (things your instruction booklet never taught you!). Fire 2: When you grab this, you automatically bring on columns of enemy ships attacking on the left and right of the screen. They're easy enough to destroy, as long as you know they're coming! Fire 4: You don't have to stay *behind* this. You can fly ahead of it and allow it to cover your flank. Fire 6, the Plasma Flash: This is a truly awesome weapon, though you'd be smart to leave it alone until the third Fortress of Area One, or the beginning of Area Two. You can't fire a new Flash until the old one has struck something and exploded. This is terrific when ships are literally raining Bombs on you: All the Flash has to do is strike one and the screen is cleared of Bombs and enemy ships. And the Bombs come fast enough so that you'll always be releasing Flashes. However, the Flash moves as slowly as a school clock; on an uncluttered screen, it's virtually useless. Another drawback to the Flash: When it blows, it takes the Boxes with it. Thus, if you're anxious to get a Chip from a Box for extra Bullets, keep your Flash holstered!

You can also get Enemy Eraser, which is released from Turrets you'll pass over. Grab this glowing ball and it'll wipe out every airborne enemy on the screen. Finally, there are the Boxes. These come at you in trios. Blast them, and if a glowing dot is released, scoop it up. That'll increase the number of Bullets you can fire—two parallel shots, three parallel shots, etc. Note: When you encounter the first trio of Boxes in any given Area (they usually appear at once), *don't* shoot them! Not a single shot! Instead, simply ram the Box in the middle. You will automatically Power-Up with triple-Bullet power! Lastly, some bad news about getting a new ship after the ZANAC you were using is destroyed. New vessels always materialize dead-center on the screen. And dead in the center is exactly what they may be; unfairly, if there's a crowd of System ships where you appear, you're going to be pulverized before you get a shot off. Life's unfair. (Note: If you gather 6 Fire 6's and then go to option, whatever characters are on the screen will become Blue Renders. Nab 'em for One-ups!)

Enemies: Most of these are detailed in the instruction booklet. Several others are discussed below. Note: While your foes always appear in the same sequence, they never appear from the same direction or at the same time or place as before. Only the Icons and Fortresses are always the same. And speaking of Fortresses—destroy one, and it'll take every enemy on the screen with it!

Menu: There is only the one-player contest.

Scoring: You earn points for destroying the System's armaments; for example, 300 points for a Terza, 1000 for a Fortress, bonuses for completing a level (10,000 for finishing Area One), etc. Note: You get points for shooting the Icons which release the Power Chips, even if you don't subsequently collect the Chip(s). Whenever you reach a Fortress (the green installations on the ground), the screen stops scrolling and you must race against a timer. The time varies as you move from Area to Area. For example, you stop at the first Fortress in Area One for 10 seconds, the first in Area Two for one minute, the first in Area Three for 45 seconds, and so on. Note: If your ship is destroyed at a Fortress, the clock does not reset when your next ship materializes.

Beginner's Strategy: In all Areas, the safest place to be is near the bottom of the screen, in the center. There are a few times when you should head upward—as when the waves of Degids or "half ships" appear left and right, then swoop toward the center of the screen to merge and attack. The phalanxes come together like a zipper, closing from the bottom up; often, they start so close to the bottom that you have no choice but to scoot to the top and stay there until they go home.

The only problems you should have in this Area are the three Fortresses. For the first: Nose right up to it and start shooting even before the clock starts. The thing should go to pieces in one second flat. When you reach the second, more powerful Fortress, go at once to the left and blast the Fire 3 Icon there. Snatch the Power Chip and position yourself just below the tiny crater beneath the center of the Fortress. Start shooting. While your Bullets chew up the Fortress, your Fire 3 power will bash the ships the Fortress sends down at you. If you only have Fire 0, not to worry—stay at the very bottom and pump the controller up. You'll rise, but so will your Bombs. When you get *too* close to the Fortress and all the bad stuff it's sending at you, slide back to the bottom and repeat. As soon as you win here, stay to the right and get Fire 7; this power is best for dealing with the last Fortress. Get up close to the computerlike box and spray it with 7 and Bullets. Not only will this take care of the Fortress, it'll zap all the ships the System sends at you. However, if you have naught but Fire 0, all is not lost. You can beat the Fortress by orbiting it very wide, literally hugging the edges of the screen and moving counterclockwise. You will be safe, here, from what it throws at you.

Note: If you have trouble with Area One, go back and try this. When the game begins and you see the battle's first Sart, shoot it using *only* Fire 0. You will earn an extra ZANAC for your arsenal!

Things speed up when you enter Area Two. The first serious enemy you'll encounter is a batlike, flickering ship that sprinkles Bombs left, right, and down. Eight of these ships usually arrive in succession (never at the same time, though), most of them appearing halfway up the screen or lower. If you don't feel like fighting them, simply get above them. If you choose to fight, Plasma Flash is your best offense. In either case, rarely will other System ships arrive until the last or second-to-last of these sleek, big vessels has appeared. Something to look out for: The instant you enter Area Two, go to the right. A Fire 3 is there, and it will be useful as you proceed; you can safely destroy the bat ship's bombs from *above* using this Power.

Area Three is actually pretty simple compared to Area Two. Reason? There's a way to become superpowerful. When you start out, stay to the right. When you spot the smiling-face Icon, blast it. You will be armed with so many weapons, you'll coast through the level. (Watch it, though. You may be armed to the teeth, but your backside is still vulnerable. All it takes is one little Bomb there to finish your fighting days.) Keep to a low, central, steady course as you cut your way through the horde of Gizas that descend. The second Fortress is X-shaped and easy to whip; so is the third. With this one, stay low (equal to the indicator in the lower right, which tells you how many ships you have left). Blast straight up with your "smile-Icon" power, and you'll destroy number three. Number-four Fortress is also a cinch. It looks like a giant tic-tac-toe board; get right up to the bottom of the square in the middle and jockey from side to side *fast.* Spray fire into the square when the doors are open, and you'll have no trouble beating it— and being whisked to Area Four.

Advanced Strategy: Things aren't so easy anymore, pilgrim! Not only will you run into a lot of ships just before you hit the first Fortress, but there are no Fire Anythings here!

To begin, shoot the two or three ships that descend, then hold your fire; the trio of Boxes comes calling next. You don't want to shoot them, you want to ram the center one for full-Bullet power. So armed, destroy the ships and two Gizas (when the latter glow red, that means they're about to die). Now, you can do one of two things. The gutsy play is on the right. Blast the small gray Turrets here, releasing their Enemy Erasers. Let those float around until you really need them; like when you see the first of the three Turrets based on the *tops* of two successive gray buildings. The Bombs they release are indestructible; if you swallow an Enemy Eraser as soon as the first building appears, the Turret is history. Blast away preemptively at the rest of the Turrets as they appear; that way, they'll only get off one shot, at the most. Next, you'll mix it up with a ton of ships. While battling these, keep sliding from side to side, or the Lusters and their steady, interminable stream of Bombs will decimate you. (They can fire up *as well as* down!) If possible, stay on the extreme left or right of the screen; the Bombs can't get you as easily here. The Fortress is up next, and it's a very baroque-looking gray and gold plus shape (+) with nine Turrets. You've got 90 seconds here; get right up to the bottom of the central, upright beam and destroy the vertical line of Turrets there. Then slide to the right and get the horizontal row of Turrets, then head left and get the emplacements there.

Of course, there's a more cowardly way to deal with the Fortress (though you'll get just as many points and stand a better chance of surviving). After you hit the first trio of Boxes and Power-Up, go to the left—not *quite* to the edge of the screen. You'll see a gray Turretless building to the right; ignore it. When the identical building appears on the left, fire up at it, at the panel on the right side of the building. Your gunfire will release a Fairy. Fly up and touch the little imp when the first of the rooftop Turrets appears. She'll light up and the Turret will explode. What's even better: When you reach the Fortress, the sprite will automatically destroy it *for* you! A long, horizontal three-Turret Fortress follows, and is easily enough destroyed.

There are eight additional levels to the game, most of them variations on Area Four: fast and full of enemy ships. Experiment as you go, firing where you might not see any enemies; like the Fairy, you never know what you'll find there—such as gates to higher levels . . . !

Par: Scores increase as you enter the higher Areas, but on average you should be able to gather 175,000 points per Area.

Training Tips: If you want to become really good, play the game without any of your Power Chip weapons. Just rocket through the System with your Bullets. That will not only increase your accuracy, but you'll learn how to maneuver like an ace to avoid what you can't destroy! Later, when you add the super weapons to your play, you'll be unstoppable!

If you want to train by jumping ahead to different levels, here's how. Put in the cartridge, turn the game on, and punch the reset button thirteen times. Hit the start button, then shift the arrow to Continue. This will enable you to choose your level.

Rating: This is like playing *Alpha Mission* with funhouse mirrors! Fast, surreal, and utterly original, *ZANAC* is a must-have game. One complaint, though: The instruction booklet was obviously written by Bubbles the chimp. "Repid-fire"? "Long time agp"? "Startted attacking"? "Ememy's"? And on the *title screen itself,* the copy reads, "game desinded by." Whew! Everyone slips up now and then, but come *on,* Nintendo! Or should that be, "Nyntendough"? Videogame players have enough trouble convincing outsiders they're not illiterate oafs. Don't compound the problem by typesetting the booklets and writing the screens with your eyes closed!

Challenge: A

Graphics: A

Sound: B

NINTENDO GAMES UPDATES

Diligent Nintendoites that we are, we've continued to play the games covered in our first book. Naturally, we've found out some new and exciting tips. Jordan Davis and Aaron Berkowitz were particularly helpful with a few of these tips to help you beat the games bad!

Zelda II—The Adventure of Link: In the fifth palace, the wall behind Ironknuckle looks solid. Not true! Beat the fiend, then walk right through the wall! (You can whip him by staying close, using Shield Magic as protection.)

Elsewhere, don't try to go after the Magic Container until you've gotten the candle from Parapa Palace. It's a waste of time and precious energy to go searching in the dark!

In the sixth palace, you'll find a boodle of locked doors . . . but no keys. How do you get in? Get the 7 magic bowls below the North Castle, at Death Mountain and Maze Island. Go to the easternmost woods and use your Hammer to whack away trees and uncover Hasuto, the hidden town. Show the old woman your bowls, and she'll give you another one. Enter a house and learn the magic spell, then head to the edge of the town. Use the spell there, and a house will rise from the ground. Enter and obtain the magic key. This will enable you to open all the locked doors!

As for that toughest of fiends, Ironknuckle, the best maneuver to use against him is to crouch, leap, and stab him. Even better: if there's an elevator handy, rise just enough to get beyond the villain's reach. When he attacks, drop and stab him. Not that Ironknuckle is all bad: whenever you encounter an Ironknuckle statue, if you stab it in the front of the helmet, the monster *may* come alive . . . or it may give you life-restoring Red Potion.

Super Mario Bros. 2: On the ice world in 4-3, you'll have to go through several mazes before you reach Fryguy . . . the boss enemy. If you want to bypass the mazes, play the Princess character. When you see the door on the bridge, pass it. Float to the other side, cross the bridge there, and there's Fryguy, in all his ugly glory.

Another terrific maneuver is for 6-3. When you've climbed the ladder, head left and walk right up to the wall . . . really put your nose against it. Your character will sink, but never fear! When you're deep enough so that your chin is just above the sand, tap the A button over and over and head left. You'll be able to crawl under the wall to the other side! You'll spot a red door here: enter, and you'll be at the pyramid which leads to Birdo.

Metroid: Input the name JUSTIN BAILEY, underline it with dashes, and enjoy the goodies with which you'll be armed!

Spy Hunter: Wouldn't it be cool to start the game with a fully-equipped car? Here's how you can begin with Oil Slicks, Smoke Screens, and Missiles. When the title screen comes up, hold down the A button, the B button, the Select button, and press down on the joystick or controller (so that it sits dead-center). Press Start, and you'll be ready to kick some fender! This code also gives you an extra life.

Mickey Mousecapade: Lost in the woods? Find your way through by traveling through the seasons. You start in the springtime. Go through the second door, and you'll be in the summer, where the trees are green. Go through the second door, to the fall. After beating the second pack of bears, leap and toss Stars at the third tree, just on the far (right) side of the break in the trees. This will enable you to head to the winter. Go right, back to the start. See the tree to the right of the sign? Jump and shoot at that tree. A magical door will appear and you'll be transported to the end of the stage.

Also, if you want to continue a game where you left off, wait until the title screen appears, then press the joystick or pad up and push the Start button.

Ikari Warriors: There's another way to jump ahead to different stages. After inputting the code listed on page 66 of our first book, wait for the screen that says Area One to appear. When it does, push the A and B buttons to shift to different stages, then press Start when you have the one you want.

Metal Gear: If you want to stop the pits from expanding in the floors of certain buildings, here's how. Hit the Select button to stop the pit from opening. Then tap the A button and go to the Weapons screen. Hit Select again. When you return to the building, the pit will have frozen in the position it was when you first stopped it. Note: the pit will *seem* to be gone, but it's still there. All you've done is stopped it from getting bigger.

And though we didn't get to cover **Simon's Quest: Castlevania II** in this book, here's a bonus, a special code you'll definitely want to try: TDLI HXDZ U48F 8TR1.

Finally, our apologies. In our last book, we said that *Joust* was for just one player. Not so! We goofed because we had just one player playing it . . . which isn't quite the same thing. Two players can enjoy it at the same time; all the same strategies apply.

Hope this whets your appetite for more games . . . because we've got 'em! Strategies for 30 new ones are coming your way in *How To Win At Nintendo Games III,* on sale in April 1990!

HOW TO
WIN
AT
NINTENDO
GAMES

Jeff Rovin

The Nintendo videogame system is the ultimate in home entertainment—an unrivaled source of excitement and challenge. And *How to Win at Nintendo Games* can help you get to the top of your form! Now packed with more vital information than ever, the new updated and expanded edition of *How to Win at Nintendo Games* covers all of your favorite games!

How to Win at Nintendo Games is an unofficial guide—not endorsed by Nintendo®. Nintendo is a registered trademark of Nintendo of America Inc.

HOW TO WIN AT NINTENDO GAMES updated edition
_____ 92018-0 $3.95 U.S.   _____ 92019-9 $4.95 Can.

**The series that redefines the meaning
of the word "*gross*"!**

*Blanche
Knott's*
Truly
Tasteless
Jokes

**Over 4 million copies of
Truly Tasteless Jokes in print!**

TRULY TASTELESS JOKES IV
_____ 90365-0 $2.95 U.S.   _____ 90366-9 $3.50 Can.

TRULY TASTELESS JOKES V
_____ 90371-5 $2.95 U.S.   _____ 90372-3 $3.50 Can.

TRULY TASTELESS JOKES VI
_____ 92130-6 $3.50 U.S.   _____ 92131-4 $4.50 Can.

TRULY TASTELESS JOKES VII
_____ 90765-6 $2.95 U.S.   _____ 90766-4 $3.95 Can.

TRULY TASTELESS JOKES VIII
_____ 91058-4 $2.95 U.S.   _____ 91059-2 $3.95 Can.

TRULY TASTELESS JOKES IX
_____ 91588-8 $3.50 U.S.   _____ 91589-6 $4.50 Can.

Publishers Book and Audio Mailing Service
P.O. Box 120159, Staten Island, NY 10312-0004

Please send me the book(s) I have checked above. I am enclosing
$ _____ (please add $1.25 for the first book, and $.25 for each
additional book to cover postage and handling. Send check or money
order only—no CODs.)

Name _____
Address _____
City _____ State/Zip _____
Please allow six weeks for delivery. Prices subject to change without
notice.

                                                    TTJ 8/89

LANDMARK
BESTSELLERS
FROM ST. MARTIN'S PRESS

HOT FLASHES
Barbara Raskin
_____ 91051-7 $4.95 U.S.   _____ 91052-5 $5.95 Can.

MAN OF THE HOUSE
"Tip" O'Neill with William Novak
_____ 91191-2 $4.95 U.S.   _____ 91192-0 $5.95 Can.

FOR THE RECORD
Donald T. Regan
_____ 91518-7 $4.95 U.S.   _____ 91519-5 $5.95 Can.

THE RED WHITE AND BLUE
John Gregory Dunne
_____ 90965-9 $4.95 U.S.   _____ 90966-7 $5.95 Can.

LINDA GOODMAN'S STAR SIGNS
Linda Goodman
_____ 91263-3 $4.95 U.S.   _____ 91264-1 $5.95 Can.

ROCKETS' RED GLARE
Greg Dinallo
_____ 91288-9 $4.50 U.S.   _____ 91289-7 $5.50 Can.

THE FITZGERALDS AND THE KENNEDYS
Doris Kearns Goodwin
_____ 90933-0 $5.95 U.S.   _____ 90934-9 $6.95 Can.

Publishers Book and Audio Mailing Service
P.O. Box 120159, Staten Island, NY 10312-0004

Please send me the book(s) I have checked above. I am enclosing
$ _____ (please add $1.25 for the first book, and $.25 for each
additional book to cover postage and handling. Send check or
money order only—no CODs.)

Name _____

Address _____

City _____ State/Zip _____

Please allow six weeks for delivery. Prices subject to change
without notice.
BEST 1/89

HERE'S HOW

HOW TO BUY A CAR by James R. Ross
The essential guide that gives you the edge in buying a new or used car.
_____ 90198-4 $3.95 U.S.   _____ 90199-2 $4.95 Can.

THE WHOLESALE-BY-MAIL CATALOG—UPDATE 1986 by The Print Project
Everything you need at 30% to 90% off retail prices—by mail or phone!
_____ 90379-0 $3.95 U.S.   _____ 90380-4 $4.95 Can.

TAKING CARE OF CLOTHES: An Owner's Manual for Care, Repair and Spot Removal by Mablen Jones
The most comprehensive handbook of its kind...save money—and save your wardrobe!
_____ 90355-3 $4.95 U.S.   _____ 90356-1 $5.95 Can.

AND THE LUCKY WINNER IS...The Complete Guide to Winning Sweepstakes & Contests
by Carolyn and Roger Tyndall with Tad Tyndall
Increase the odds in your favor—all you need to know.
_____ 90025-2 $3.95 U.S.   _____ 90026-0 $4.95 Can.

THE OFFICIAL HARVARD STUDENT AGENCIES BARTENDING COURSE
The new complete guide to drinkmaking—the $40 course now a paperback book!
_____ 90427-4 $3.95 U.S.   _____ 90430-4 $4.95 Can.